From Grief to Memories

Kei Gilbert, M.A.
Thanatologist

ISBN #: 0-9650386-3-7

Soras Corporation
12506 White Drive
Silver Spring, Maryland 20904

Web site: http://www.soras.com

$\mathscr{T}$ABLE OF CONTENTS

Let grief find
the freedom to be expressed

Let grief find
the right to be understood

KEI GILBERT

$\mathcal{A}$CKNOWLEDGMENTS

Some profound thoughts and creativity are born or discovered at difficult times in our lives. Divorce is one of those times. Grief of losing someone to death is another. Our thoughts, however, often remain on the pages of a private diary or are soon forgotten as we move on to happier times. Worse yet, we sometimes forget to notice those around us who are grieving over their new losses.

There are yet times when we sense a strong conviction that the given understanding must be shared. This book, as with other books, began with a raw inspiration felt with my heart, not yet expressed in words. I was able to explore and fine-tune those thoughts with uninhibited creativity only with the help of friends and family who recognized the value of this book and helped me develop it into what you now see in print.

I believe that "guardian angels" exist within our reach and touch. They have flown through the hands and the hearts of the following people to enable me to complete this book.

$\mathcal{M}$Y ANGELS

Inspiration:	My mother from her heavenly world
	My "guardian angels" who didn't let me quit
Cherished support:	My husband, Michael, for his sacrifices
	Joanne Kimura, for being there
	Roberta Rook, Jan Madden, and Sue Adams
	for their encouragement
	Classmates, friends and family for their
	understanding and patience

Knowledge:	Drs. Cable, Martin, and Ruffin for their commitment to the Thanatology Program at Hood College
Charcoal Drawing:	Linda Craven, for beautifully enhancing my drawings
Technical Editing:	Roberta Rook, my savior
Editing:	Linda Anderson
	Liz Castro
	Pat Connolly
	Muriel Pitman Craven
	Michael Gilbert
	Joanne Kimura
	Romona and Seymour Rottenberg
	Linda Simmons
	Carolyn Taylor
	Margaret Zierdt
Inspirational messages:	Susan Adams
	Deborah Boggs
	Cathy Campbell
	Trisha Kiyohara
	Lauren MacBlane
	Pastor Ray (Scheck)
	Roberta Rook
	Linda Scott

*I hope to dedicate the rest of my life to the communication of love, especially when grief is at hand. If you would like to contribute your writing or thoughts to be included in the next edition, please contact me through **www.soras.com**.*

Kei Gilbert

$\mathcal{F}$OREWORD

For better or worse, grief is a universal experience. In life, we are faced with the death or a loss of a significant relationship. Each of these deaths impacts us in ways that will stay with us throughout life. It would seem then that we should all understand the grief that others experience. However, it is not that simple.

Every relationship has a uniqueness to it. For example, each of us may relate to a parent in the parent-child role. But how that relationship is carried forth, and the impact it has in our lives is different for everyone. With the end of a relationship, the grief that follows carries its uniqueness. There is really no way to compare the grief that two individuals experience over a seemingly similar loss.

The one common aspect of our grief experiences is that each death or loss of a relationship requires a "working through" of the relationship, the loss experience, and an orientation toward a future without that person as an active part of our life. It is this "working through the grief" that is sometimes very difficult for us. Some of us have the capacity and ability to do it all on our own with our own inner strength, spiritualism, or other personal tools. Others need a strong support system to help them. Still others may need the assistance of a professional grief therapist.

For those of us who have worked with grievers over the years, perhaps the one amazing thing we see is that despite the pain of grief and how it tears the human being apart, ultimately, most grievers come through the process and are stronger human beings than they ever believed they could be. Time and again, we listen to those grievers who have no desire to go on with life, only to see them emerge and move on in healthy, positive ways. Once

From Grief to Memories

they learn that they never have to forget the person, they find that they can put their loved one in a new "place" where, from time to time, they can remember with good feelings, the relationship that they once cherished.

A significant mistake that many grievers make is in believing that "time heals all." The reality is that time does nothing but pass. The healing takes place by our actively working through the relationship and the feelings we have. To do this, we need a variety of methods to help us.

This workbook provides an excellent tool that can assist grievers as they strive to understand their grief and find a way to incorporate the memories of the person into their lives. The grievers can find materials and methods to help with the long journey they are undertaking through inspirational material, exercises, perspectives on the grief experience, and reflections from those who have made this journey before.

As you make this journey, recognize that you are not alone and that all of us in the human race have been where you are now and will be again. May the following pages make your journey a little easier and more meaningful to you.

Dana Cable, Ph.D.
Professor of Psychology,
Hood College
Grief Counselor
January 7, 2001

NTRODUCTION

On February 15, 1999, I lost my mother to a sudden and traumatic death. I had gone to Seattle to help her at the hospital as she was having gastrointestinal problems. While I was there, in six days, we went from worrying over the cause, preparing her for a major surgery, celebrating over her great recovery, preparing for her to be discharged, and then suddenly watching her die from hemorrhaging. Those were the most intense six days of my life, and it has taken me months to overcome the lasting image of her disfigured body and the violent death, so contrary to her quiet and peaceful nature.

At her deathbed, I promised that I would write a beautiful book on her life entitled, *Katsuko, the Winning Child.* Her parents had named her "the winning child" at birth, and she lived and died as a winner. Two years after her death, I am writing a different book, dedicating it to her life.

Being the only child meant I had no siblings with whom I could share this grief. Living on the opposite coast also meant that friends here really didn't know my mother well. Most of my family and friends who knew her were all far away. It was a lonely world. I struggled the first year, but oddly enough, I had enrolled in school prior to her death to become certified in thanatology (psychology of death and dying), so my studies on grief served not only to provide me with a graduate degree but to assist me with my own grief.

I was searching for an answer to one question last year: *What can I do to help those who lack a strong support system for dealing with their grief?* Do I become a therapist? Do I become a lecturer? Or do I write again? I first began designing a grief kit — a memory box and an album — using my wood-burning tools. Then I decided that a good workbook and a videotape would be needed in addition to those items.

This workbook is based on my own experience with grief, seen from the point of view of what I needed to do to go from trauma to positive memories. It was further enriched by the concepts learned in the thanatology program and by the comforting words of others. The book, I hope, will give you some choices in how you handle your own grief. It's a box of chocolates on grief. Choose the pieces that fit your needs.

I went through three vague phases to process my grief: (1) I first "sensed or felt" my loss and associated emotions through a period of blurred vision; (2) I strained my raw emotions through a sieve and used personalized rituals to further break down the lumps; (3) I then read to understand the grieving process universal to everyone. At the onset of my mother's death, with all the emotions associated with the loss, I was not in the right frame of mind to read textbooks on why we grieve. I could, however, look at nature, photographs or drawings and express my feelings on life and death. This workbook, therefore, is organized so that those who have lost their loved ones can deal with their grief on their appropriate or chosen level through drawings, poems, writing, memorializing, or reading about what death and grief are all about. The workbook is thus organized into the following five sections, based on the three basic phases mentioned above:

Section I: DRIFTING THOUGHTS:

At the time of death of a loved one, physical or mental, we may be too exhausted and too numb to want to read. I chose the first section to include some sketches and poetic pages. There is no need to do any heavy thinking. Instead, look at the sketches and ponder on the words on the adjacent page. They are the thoughts and images I had during my grief period on life and death. I hope you will find some comfort while reading them. A loss, while it is painful, can give you opportunities to evaluate life.

Section II: TALKING, WRITING, DOING:

Death or a loss of someone significant in your life ignites such a range of reactions. If we simply did nothing but ponder about the "what, why, and how" of life's events, grief can stay with us for many years. The following exercises will help you chip away some of your grief:

1. Misconceptions
2. Exploring your emotions
3. Evaluating your stress level
4. Your past losses
5. Your support system
6. Your regrets
7. Forgiving
8. Creative tools
9. Memorializing
10. Holidays
11. A time for a change

In other words, each death affects us in different ways, and we must seek our own appropriate ways to turn sorrow into positive memories. Ceremonial acts, such as funerals and memorial services, provide opportunities to memorialize the deceased, which is a very important process of letting go. In the last few decades, we have spent less and less time devoted to memorializing our losses. We are forgetting that it is really not so much for the deceased but for us that we memorialize. These "grief tasks" help us release our strong, built-up emotions. We can do this through writing, playing music, drawing, planning ceremonial exercises, talking, gardening or other activities that are special to us.

From Grief to Memories

Section III: UNDERSTANDING:

This section will cover the following topics:

1. Historical aspect on death and grief
2. The grief process
3. Grief tasks
4. Types of death
5. Difficult death
6. Grief styles
7. Awareness levels
8. Grief symptoms
9. Complicated grief
10. Disenfranchised grief
11. Children and the elderly
12. Pet loss
13. Multicultural interest

Since Elisabeth Kübler-Ross popularized the study of death and dying in this century, others have continued to study the complex but universal experience called "death." One aspect of death is how each of us responds when someone we love dies. This response is grief. This section will summarize some of the current understanding of how similarly or differently we grieve, from children to the elderly, and from one culture to another. I hope that you will research on your own to study further the areas that interest you.

Section IV: COMFORTING WORDS:

This is a collection of writings contributed by those who have gone through grief. They have written from their heart to share their experiences with you.

Section V: $\mathcal{R}$ESOURCES:

This section provides a short list of books, films and organizations which may of interest to you.

Coping with grief is a life-long process. Your friends who have not had any profound experience with a significant loss may not understand how you can miss someone for so many years. It is OK to have these feelings. It simply shows that you, at one point, had a very meaningful relationship with that person. I hope that this workbook will allow you to give yourself the right to have those feelings and to express them. You may wrestle with the question, "What if I had done . . ." when someone significant in your life suddenly dies. There may be unfinished or unresolved work that surfaces after someone dies. So death brings to you not only sadness but a bag of mixed emotions that need to be worked out.

If you are reading this book because you have just lost someone you loved, this book cannot remove your sadness from your life. It can, however, provide you with some tools that will enable you to cope with your grief. I hope you will feel my heartfelt empathy and my sincere wishes that tomorrow will be a little easier day for you.

Kei Gilbert

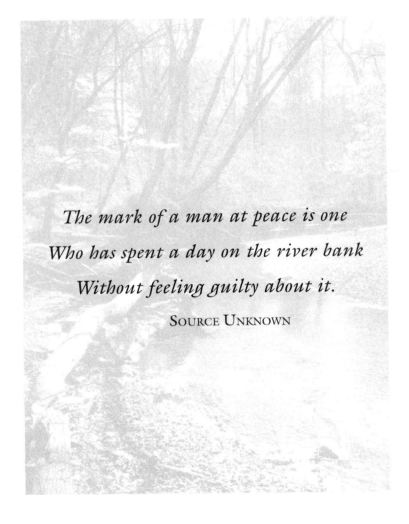

The mark of a man at peace is one
Who has spent a day on the river bank
Without feeling guilty about it.

SOURCE UNKNOWN

Section I:

DRIFTING THOUGHTS

I am sharing the following poems and sketches conceived during the two difficult years of grief to prove that it doesn't take an established poet or an artist to play with creativity. If I can do it, so can you! Art and writing are great tools for expressing feelings.

Wisdom begins in wonder.

SOCRATES

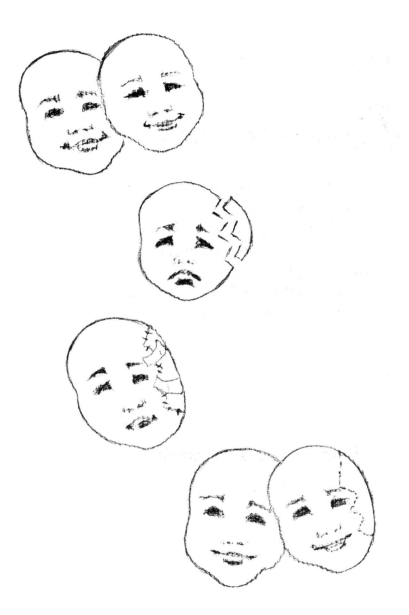

(This concept was introduced by Dr. Terry Martin)

THE LOSS OF AN IMPORTANT RELATIONSHIP

When someone we love suddenly leaves us
> There is rawness in the tear
>> Jaggedness of the pain within us

When someone we love is gone from our touch
> We feel lost and stunned
>> That a part of us went with our beloved

When someone we love has been gone for a while
> We begin to let that wound heal itself
>> Aided by invisible stitches our soul provides

When someone we love is missed
> We let time and friends be our best guides
>> To replace the void with new joys of life

When someone we love is remembered
> We are replacing our sorrow with memories
>> To let the healed scars honor the life we shared

 IMONO

I watched my grandmother, in postwar Japan, carefully taking her kimono strips apart to wash and stretch them out to dry between two lines in the sun. Even as a child, I was amazed at how her kimono with a perfect shape turned into little strips that were sewn back up to regain its shape. Most of the time, I saw no difference in her kimono, except that she knew it was clean. Sometimes, there was a strip here and there that had been replaced.

A death or a loss of someone in our life is just like that — taking our shapely kimono into pieces and sewing them back up again: Cleaning. Stretching. Drying. Reconnecting. My grandmother knew that her kimono would soon find its shape again. She had outlived four of her children before she died at age 84. She must have known how to take her sorrow apart into strips, clean them, stretch them out, dry them, and reconnect them again and again.

A JUG OF WATER RETURNS HOME

There is a scene in a classic movie called "A Houseboat" where a father finds a way to explain the death of a mother to a young boy. The father empties out the water in the jug into the body of water surrounding the houseboat. He tells the boy that just like the way the water in the jug became part of the bigger body of water, his mother's soul was still living in the bigger stream of life.

*T*HE GLASSES THAT DON'T FIT

One of the trying moments in grief is when friends surprise you with advice that makes you feel worse.

When my mother died, I received a note from a friend saying that because I was strong and self-assured, everything would be OK. Was she talking about me — a lost soul who did nothing but cry day after day? The same friend said that she kept distance from me because she needed to be alone when her husband died. What I needed, though, was a friend who would simply cry with me.

How often do we receive "sympathy words" contrary to our needs? It is as if someone is giving us corrective lenses too strong for our eyes. We are blinded by their strength. Astigmatism. Near-sightedness. Far-sightedness. Behind the pair of eyes that see the world through rods and cones, our sight on life is as varied as our vision. Can my lenses for astigmatism correct your far-sightedness? Can my bifocals correct your blurred vision? Are my lenses too weak or too strong for you? Are my comments appropriate for you? The best support we can give and receive, perhaps, is a simple reassurance of love and support that no words can convey.

We don't always find the right glasses that fit during the early days of grief. Be patient. Soon enough, you will have the urge to see again, and you will go out looking for the right pair of glasses made just for you.

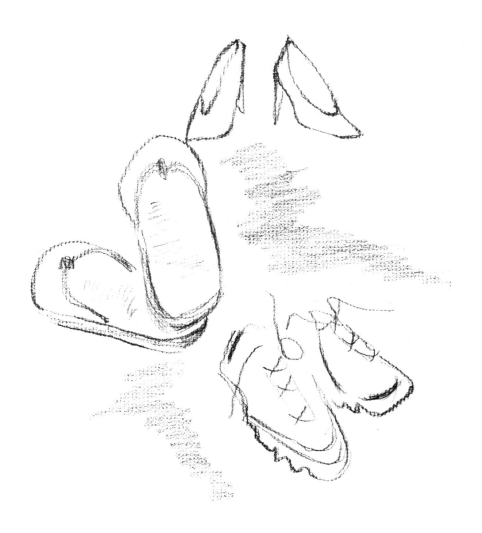

*Y*OUR SHOES

What do you do when you want to play tennis today?

No, you won't wear your ice-hockey skates.

What do you do when you want to go dancing?

No, you won't wear your favorite hiking boots.

What do you do when the rain turns to snow?

No, you won't wear your vinyl beach sandals.

What do you do when your shoe has a hole?

No, you won't mend it with masking tape.

What do you do when you've lost someone dear?

You will look for the right shoes to walk.

Comfortable yet strong . . .

Flexible yet protective . . .

Airy yet powerful . . .

It may take a while to find the right fit,

But life is a process of trying on shoes, isn't it?

SIMPLIFYING

The kitchen is full of utensils I hardly ever use
    I can't find my chopsticks that Grandma gave me

The bathroom is full of make-up and brushes
    I can't find the new toothpaste I bought the other day

The office is crammed with old files
    I can't understand who wrote what

The yard is full of new and old plants
    I can't separate the flowers from the weeds

The pillar of my life suddenly leaves
    and I can't see beyond the debris around me

It's time to simplify . . .
    to find my chopsticks, toothpaste, the right file
    and to recognize the important friends who are
    waiting for me

Drifting Thoughts

RECYCLING

Old smashed coke cans become clean, new cans

Today's newspaper becomes tomorrow's stationery

Rotten tree stumps become future mulch

Discarded grass from the yard becomes tomorrow's nutrients

Our sorrow can become tomorrow's understanding

*M*y **WRINKLES**

My favorite trusted name-brand shirt
    Refused to sparkle without a press

The freshly ironed business shirt
    Hid in the closet without a wrinkle

Today I looked at myself in the bathroom mirror
    To examine the lines on my aging face

What I saw though were the wrinkles in my spirit
    From the wear and tear of yesterday's race

Too absorbed was I by the weariness of grief
    To see life hidden beneath the sunken look

Immobilized by the glance of my dying face
    I smiled at the mirror to see if the face was real

The mirror suddenly lit up
    As if the smile were alive

I then grabbed my iron
    And pressed on my wrinkled soul

Out I went determined
    To run another mile

Drifting Thoughts

*I*T'S TIME TO SAVE AGAIN

Sometimes

    Our piggy bank is growing

Sometimes

    Our piggy bank is bulging

Sometimes

    Our piggy bank gets emptied

Sometimes

    Our piggy bank has no reserve

Sometimes

    We need to start all over again

Drifting Thoughts

$\mathcal{A}$ HOLE IN MY HEART

One day, my daughter asked me,
>"Am I always going to have a hole in my heart
>for a father I never had?"

I looked at her in silence then,
>since I had no answer to give.

One day, I asked myself the same question,
>"Am I always going to have a hole in my heart
>for the mother I just lost?"

Yes, I can now say,
>the holes will always be there.

Yes, but I can also say,
>the holes will not always drain our spirit
>and we will learn to accept their existence.

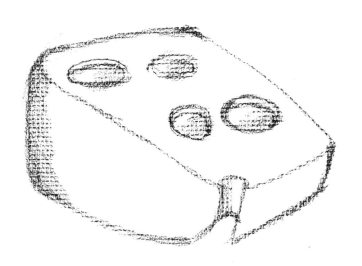

$\mathcal{S}$WISS CHEESE

Swiss cheese is what life is all about.
>It grows holes within as it ages with time
>>As if less is better than more in weight.
>Its flavor grows in time
>>As if aging makes it more interesting.
>It stays firm in spite of lost space
>>As if through our losses we find more courage.

"What else?" do you say.
>Why, of course, it makes the best omelette!
>>To make eggs, its bland companion,
>>>Gain some extra spunk.

So be the best Swiss cheese you can be
>In spite of the holes deemed negative in some eyes
>>Finding beauty and strength to hold on its own.

Drifting Thoughts

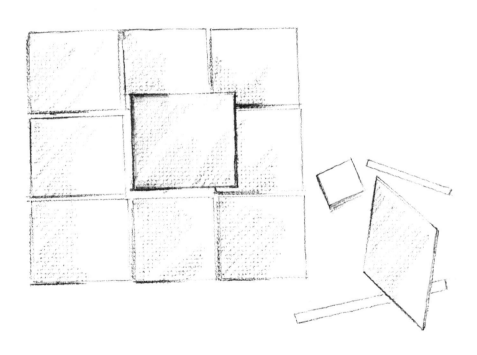

REPLACING TILES

I was placing linoleum tiles on the kitchen floor. Everything seemed easy until I came to a corner where the tiles needed to be cut. I cut one piece. It was slightly too big. I cut another, and it was slightly too small. I traced the area and cut another piece. It still didn't fit. Finally, after many tries, I managed to fill most of the gap. It wasn't perfect, but it did the job.

Sometimes, when we lose a relationship, it's hard to fill the gap that it leaves behind. As with the tiles, we seem to keep on trying to find a replacement piece until we make it fit. If we're lucky, it's a perfect fit. Sometimes, we try until we're satisfied, accepting the imperfections in the replacement tile.

$\mathcal{A}$ LONG HIKE

One day I was told to go on a hike the next morning.

I got ready to go for the day.

    I looked for good walking shoes
    and packed a lunch with drinks.

Then someone said that it could rain.

    "Rain gear," I said, and I packed my yellow raincoat.

Then someone said that it could be a long hike,

    So I packed a blanket, soap and a washcloth.

Then someone said that there were no guides,

    So I packed a road map and a flashlight.

Then someone said that it could be cold at night

    So I packed some matches and paper to take.

Then someone said that no one ever came back to tell.

Then I looked at my
    Shoes
    Food and drinks
    Rain gear
    Blanket
    Soap and washcloth
    Road Map
    Flashlight
    Matches and paper

"Will all this be enough," I asked myself.

Then I asked that someone, "Will I be alone?"

    That someone said,

    "Yes, but don't be afraid.
    There are friends waiting for you
    at the end of the hike."

Drifting Thoughts

 A TURBULENT RIVER

The hurricane brought wind and rain
> and the river was now chocolate mousse

I went searching for my special colorful pebbles
> stored in the densely wooded bank

My arm swung gently in the dark murky water
> but it found only some mud and sharp broken sticks

I waited several days and returned to see the river
> with crystal clear water where sand had settled
> > to the bottom

Gently I scooped up the river bed again
> and the colorful pebbles met me with their usual
> > show of glee

Time had quieted down the turbulent, muddy river
> and restored it to its tranquil comforting face

RUNING

Sometimes
it takes losing important limbs
to see the rejuvenated life emerge

I was all ready to dump the dying bushes
as there was very little life left
in their frail silhouettes

I took my saw and pruned with brute force
hoping that with a clean fresh start
a new life might somehow emerge

One day I saw small young leaves
dancing like elves atop the low stumps
giving promises of great adulthood

Then I knew
that sometimes
it takes cutting down all the way
to see the essence of life waiting to be exposed

A KITE THAT FLEW AWAY

A strong wind made my kite thrust forward
    and I could feel its intensity
        as it stretched out by a line of thread

Looking around
    there were many others
        paralleling my kite toward the authoritative wind

Snap, I felt the line clip in half
    and what I had left in my hand
        was a short lifeless string

I watched my kite being carried away
    as if saying good-bye
        to its well-wishers left behind

Where are you going?
    I yelled at my kite
        but it disappeared before it could say a word

I looked at my friends
    still holding on to their strings
        but I noticed that we no longer had a shared goal

I'm so sorry!
    yelled out one friend
        but I didn't know what to do with my lifeless string

Drifting Thoughts

$\mathcal{P}$LANTING MY GARDEN

Tulips in vibrant colors give several weeks of joy
    But May brings an end to their colorful display

Lilacs bring a sweet scent in the early hours of spring
    But lilacs alone leave the summer months looking
    quite bare

Hydrangeas bloom in June with their brushes widely spread
    But August brings an end to their dazzling fireworks

Roses bring an endless mix of colors and smell
    But the deer can eat them during their early morning stroll

Maples flash burning colors in the brisk autumn months
    But November leaves the branches empty and bare

Perennials return with growth year after year
    But the acts of nature can threaten their expected return

Annuals flaunt lavishly in the sun-filled summer
    But their stay is quite temporary as they forget to return

So gardening is an art of knowing what and when to plant
    Ensuring the flow of joy throughout the entire year

Life, too, is an art of knowing what and when to plant
    For seeking a quick relief may not bring tomorrow's joy

Life, too, is a matter of being patiently waiting
    For today's hard work will bring tomorrow's delight

Drifting Thoughts

SUNSETS AND SUNRISES

Each sunset
casts a shadow on me
to release, reflect, and review my vision

> and in its total darkness
> where my shadow speaks out loud
> I see what I could have done

Each sunrise
erases yesterday's doubts
to refresh, renew, and resew my vision

> and in its brightness
> with my path cleared of debris
> I see what I can touch

In the shadow, we learn to see
and in brightness, we learn to touch

> each day bringing us new chances for growth
> to turn pain into spring flowers
> and joy to fertilize new seedlings of hope

Drifting Thoughts

A man dies many times
as he loses a loved one.

SYRUS

Section II:

Talking...
Writing...
Doing...

Three tools of dealing with grief

Give sorrow words.

WILLIAM SHAKESPEARE

45

Those who do not know how to weep with their whole heart don't know how to laugh either.

GOLDA MEIR

WHAT THIS SECTION COVERS

This section goes beyond "Drifting Thoughts" in that you will focus more on your feelings. You will be in the "talking, writing and doing" stage of grief. The following topics will be covered:

1. *Misconceptions*

2. *Exploring Emotions*

3. *Evaluating Your Stress Level*

4. *Your Past Losses*

5. *Your Support System*

6. *Regrets and Unfinished Business*

7. *Forgiving*

8. *Creative Tools*

9. *Memorializing*

10. *Holidays*

11. *A Time for a Change*

The greater the obstacle,
the more glory
in overcoming it.

MOLIÈRE

1. Misconceptions

The following are misconceptions.
Directions: *Put check marks next to those you believe.*

☐ ***"I should work hard to ignore my sadness."***
Suppressing grief will only prolong its duration, and it can one day strike you unexpectedly. It's like leaving the water on with the sprinkler knob turned off. It may burst the hose or shock you with its force once you turn the knob on.

☐ ***"It was a 'good death.' I shouldn't have negative feelings."***
There are usually unfinished thoughts or actions and memories of spoken and unspoken words that can haunt you after someone dies. A parent dies from a painless, sudden death after struggling with a chronic illness. What if you had wished the week before that he (she) would die quickly with no pain? Emotions play a big part during the grieving process. It's natural to have those thoughts. One day, you can see the logic behind them.

☐ ***"I should show my strength by not crying in public."***
Crying is a sign of the tension within you and that you cared deeply for someone. A quote by Washington Irving: "There is a sacredness in tears. They are not the mark of weakness, but of power. They speak more eloquently than 10,000 tongues. They are the messengers of overwhelming grief, of deep contrition and of unspeakable love."

☐ **"My faith should take care of my grief."**
Spirituality will certainly help you with your sense of loss. Grief, however, is a show of human emotions, not a show of how religious one is in life.

☐ **"We all grieve in the same way. I should try to be like my sister who's being stoic."**
Our grief is affected by so many things. For example, by the timing of the loss (both for you and the loved one), your past relationship, the nature of the loss, your reservoir of strength, your health, your spirituality, your support system, your personality, your culture, etc. We all grieve differently.

☐ **"I should get over my grief in a few months."**
Grief has no timing. Even those who seem to have found inner peace may be unexpectedly hit by a resurgence of grief symptoms in the distant future. Usually, it takes repeated anniversaries of special events, without the loved one sharing the experience, to gradually become adjusted to the new life. Grief can surprise you, however, years later at unexpected moments.

☐ **"I shouldn't have bad feelings about a dead person."**
The deceased can't hurt you any more in a new way, but your old feelings can. There may have been unfinished business that still causes anger in you. You have the right to have those emotions. Allow yourself to feel them, and then try to work them out.

2. Exploring Emotions

WHAT EMOTIONS DO I HAVE?

Losing someone special can bring about a myriad of emotions, which are often not understood or dismissed. Let's talk about them.

I'm sad because:

_____

_____

_____

_____

_____

I'm angry because:

_____

_____

_____

_____

_____

I'm happy because:

_____

_____

_____

_____

_____

Talking, Writing, Doing

I feel relieved because:

_____

_____

_____

_____

_____

_____

I feel frustrated because:

_____

_____

_____

_____

_____

_____

I feel guilty because:

_____

_____

_____

_____

_____

_____

You might be surprised that you have happy feelings about one aspect of your loss in spite of the fact that you feel you should be "grieving." Write those feelings down. You also may have a sense of guilt over how you could have saved the situation, whether the possibility is real or not. Write those feelings down. You will notice that the loss you're experiencing has not only sadness but other emotions attached to it. So you're human! We are complex in the way we view ourselves and the world around us.

Talking, Writing, Doing

MY FEELINGS

Directions: *Circle or highlight the feeling you have and connect it to the center picture representing you.*

He's not in pain now.

I could have done more.

It's not fair.

I have to look strong.

He'll be disappointed in me if I . . .

It's the doctor's fault!

Why me?

How much more would it cost?

It can't be happening to me!

I sort of feel relieved . . .

At least I have my life back.

This shouldn't have happened.

I feel peaceful.

Pretty flowers.

No one loves me.

I wish I had seen her (him) once more.

I should have done that.

I miss him (her).

I don't feel sad.

She wasn't a real friend.

I'm mad at my family.

My friend didn't call me.

It's my turn next.

It hurts.

My sister is selfish.

Why did it happen to me?

How much more can I carry?

He only thinks about himself.

Why did I say that?

I feel numb.

I feel so lonely.

Why did he (she) die before me?

He (she) was in so much pain . . .

Why, why, why?

Did I make that happen?

Everyone's forgotten about me.

Why didn't he (she) send me a card?

Why aren't they grieving?

3. Evaluating Your Stress Level

SO YOU ARE STRESSED OUT?

The emotions that accompany a significant loss use up a lot of energy. It can be difficult when you already have little water left in your well. Let's look at your current stress in your life — both physical and mental. It helps to understand why you are feeling overwhelmed.

Directions: *Evaluate your physical and mental conditions prior to the loss.*

Rate between 1 - 10, with 1 meaning least significant. Write the number on the line provided.

Your physical and mental conditions: *1 2 3 4 5 6 7 8 9 10*

- ◆ Stomach/gastrointestinal problems   _____
- ◆ Headaches   _____
- ◆ Backaches   _____
- ◆ Joint/muscle aches   _____
- ◆ Fatigue   _____
- ◆ Sleeping problems   _____
- ◆ Depression   _____
- ◆ Psychological disorder   _____

Stress from your work: *1 2 3 4 5 6 7 8 9 10*

- ◆ From your co-workers   _____
- ◆ From your bosses   _____
- ◆ From the workload   _____
- ◆ From boredom   _____

Stress from your family:

1 2 3 4 5 6 7 8 9 10

- ◆ Your spouse   _____
- ◆ Your children   _____
- ◆ Your parents   _____
- ◆ Your sibling   _____
- ◆ Pets   _____
- ◆ Others   _____

Stress related to financial worries:

1 2 3 4 5 6 7 8 9 10

- ◆ About yourself   _____
- ◆ About your children/spouse   _____
- ◆ About your parents/others   _____

Stress from relationships:

1 2 3 4 5 6 7 8 9 10

- ◆ Significant others   _____
- ◆ Neighbors   _____
- ◆ Co-workers/bosses   _____
- ◆ Church groups   _____

Personal issues:

1 2 3 4 5 6 7 8 9 10

- ◆ Concerns over personal growth   _____
- ◆ Worries over spirituality   _____

For every stress or condition that is 5 or above, color the *small circles* red on page 57. Don't fret over having many red spots. Life would not be interesting if we didn't have stress. We are just trying to understand how much water you need to put in your well.

4. Your Past Losses

DEATH EXPERIENCE:

Directions: *At this time, focus on what other losses you have had in your life: (Put a big check if it was a sudden or traumatic death.)*

Death of family members:

1. _____
2. _____
3. _____
4. _____
5. _____
6. _____
7. _____
8. _____

Death of friends and co-workers:

1. _____
2. _____
3. _____
4. _____
5. _____
6. _____
7. _____
8. _____

Death of neighbors or public figures you respected:

1. _____

2. _____

3. _____

4. _____

5. _____

EXPERIENCES IN THE RECENT YEARS:

Divorce/separation: _____

Miscarriage/abortion: _____

Unemployment: _____

Demotion: _____

Business failure: _____

Relocation (residence): _____

Pet loss: _____

Car accident: _____

Assault/burglary: _____

Loss of health: _____

Other losses: _____

If you have had a lot to write on these two pages, it means that you have had your share of challenges in your life. These past challenges may have taught you how to deal with this recent loss. However, most of us have some work left over from our past, and the residue can add up to make our current situation more complex and tough to handle.

Now you will go back to page 57 and add more color to this picture. When it is finished, you will have a symbolic view of the challenges in your life.

Directions:

For each entry you had in this section, color the big circles in red. For example, if you had 3 entries under "Death experiences" and 2 under "Experiences in recent years," you color 5 big red circles.

Being aware of your past and present sources of stress — what you've endured and what you're facing now — can help you understand the current level of your emotions.

Only the wearer knows where the shoe pinches.

ENGLISH PROVERB

5. Your Support System

> *Blessed is the influence*
> *of one true, loving*
> *human soul on another.*
>
> GEORGE ELIOT

Fools are those who believe that they are capable of living their lives through self-reliance alone. Sometimes, we are dealt with more challenges than we know how to handle, and it's friends, family and strangers who come into our life to help. I call them "life's sweeteners." Some come as powdered sugar, some in granules, and some even in form of cubes. They can be white, shades of brown or even colored red and green. Some are obnoxious in their potent sugary taste, and others are hardly noticeable, as in peanut butter or ketchup.

As in real sugar, life's sweeteners come in different forms. Although books and tapes can certainly give you support, they often cannot replace the human touch — words, hugs and a pat on the back. Let's now look at your support system. Do you have strong support? If not, be optimistic because it is not difficult to create your own.

SUPPORT CAN COME FROM THE FOLLOWING EXAMPLE GROUPS:

Family:	Mother	Aunts and uncles
	Father	Grandparents
	Siblings	Cousins
	Children	Distant relatives
Friends:	Old and new friends:	
	Classmates	Church friends
	Co-workers	Neighbors
	Mailman	Familiar store clerks
Services:	Counselor	Church
	Hospital-sponsored	Community-sponsored
	support groups	support groups
	Hospice	
Strangers:	Anyone who comes in contact with you can "kindle your spirit."	

CONSULTING THE LIST ABOVE, WRITE DOWN NAMES OF THOSE WHO CAN HELP.

1. Those who will come to you WITHOUT BEING ASKED:

_____

_____

_____

_____

2. *Those who willingly will come if you ask them to come:*

_____

_____

_____

3. *Those who will call to see if you're OK:*

_____

_____

_____

4. *Those who will listen to you if you called:*

_____

_____

_____

5. *A counselor or a physician you can see:*

_____

_____

_____

6. *Support groups you can join (religious or secular):*

_____

_____

_____

Talking, Writing, Doing

7. *Strangers who might "kindle your spirit:"*
   (Where would you go to be in contact with people? For
   example, a park, a shopping mall, a computer store.)

   _____

   _____

   _____

   (My support list was initially thin for my own grief, but I
   found a lot of unexpected support through the kind
   gestures and smiles that came from strangers.)

SOME ADVICE:

1. *Don't stay a victim!*
   It's easy to become and stay a victim when you sense that no
   one else cares enough about your feelings. Seek
   opportunities to express your feelings and then find a
   positive direction for your new life without the loved one.

2. *Spread around your "verbalizing" to more than one
   person.*
   Your friend may love you a lot and want to support you, but
   constant retelling of the same story can get old. If you have
   heavy unloading to do, spread it around to many people so
   you can get your needed support.

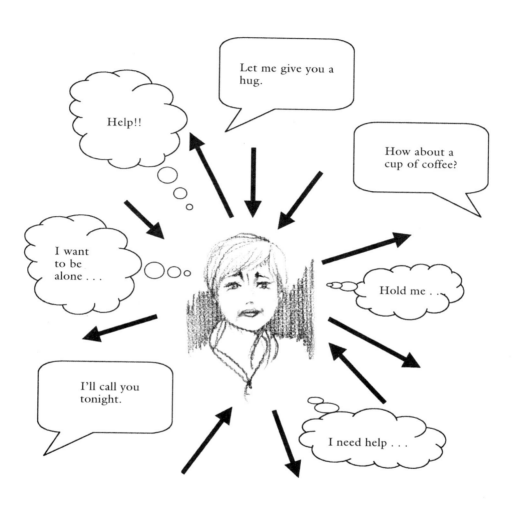

65

*Sometimes our light goes out
but is blown into flame
by another human being.*

*Each of us owes deepest thanks
to those who have
rekindled this light.*

ALBERT SCHWEITZER

6. Regrets and Unfinished Business

When my mother died from a sudden and unexpected death, I should have had no sense of guilt since I spent six sleepless nights at the hospital, being the best advocate I could be. I was surprised that I had a sense of guilt when she died. My mother had been on cortisone for 50 years for asthma and rheumatoid arthritis, and she had lived a life challenged with physical ailments. A few years ago, I had thought, "I hope she goes quickly one day." That thought resurfaced from my memory after her death, in spite of my earnest effort to help her extend her life. I felt guilty that I had actually thought about a "quick death" for her so that she would not suffer so much. "Did I will it to happen?" I asked myself. Reason does not always prevail at the time of a traumatic event. If you are having those remorseful moments, give yourself some room to express those feelings to a friend or on paper. Then tell yourself that you didn't cause the death (or the loss). This act of "forgiving oneself" is a powerful tool for moving from grief to positive memories.

THE FOLLOWING SPACE IS RESERVED FOR YOUR REGRETS.

I feel guilty that . . .

_____

_____

_____

_____

_____

_____

_____

_____

Talking, Writing, Doing

I regret not having done:

_____

_____

_____

_____

_____

_____

_____

_____

_____

_____

I regret not having said:

_____

_____

_____

_____

_____

_____

_____

_____

_____

_____

_____

A LETTER TO THE LOVED ONE

Directions: *Writing is a very good release for expressing emotions. Tell your loved one exactly how you feel. Express all of your emotions, including anger, jealousy, regrets, guilt, a sense of relief, happiness, etc.*

What death or a loss can do to you

A loss of something special can cripple love.
    But you have the power to mend that love.

It can shatter hope.
    But you have the power to reconstruct that hope.

It can corrode faith.
    But time can reinstate that faith in you.

It can suppress a sense of humor.
    But laughter will return in time.

It can destroy inner peace.
    But time will bring you back to that peace.

It can kill friendships.
    But new friends are waiting around the corner.

It can suppress memories.
    But time will unveil them again.

It can silence courage.
    But it will find its voice again.

It can invade the soul.
    But it cannot destroy its ability to cleanse itself.

It can seemingly conquer your spirit,
    But search for the love at the bottom of your well,
    For you will be blanketed with the softness of that love.

(Concept based on *"What cancer cannot do,"*
author unknown)

DIRECTED IMAGERY

When someone dies, that person takes with him all the future possibilities of communication. We so often think, "If only I had said . . . before he (she) died." You might wish you had said "I love you" more openly. Perhaps the deceased was too young to die. Perhaps, in a dysfunctional relationship, it was too painful for you to discuss any of your buried feelings with that person before he or she died. That person has moved on, but the memory of a dysfunctional relationship or unfinished business related to your relationship with him or her remains alive within you. Does it mean that you will bear the burden of carrying that weight for the rest of your life? No, but time alone might not relieve you of your burden. There are several things you can do.

1. ***Empty Chair:***

    Place a chair in a quiet area of the house where you will not be disturbed. If you'd like, light a candle and put some soothing music in the background. Then begin talking to the deceased as if he or she is sitting on that chair. Say anything and everything you want to say. Don't hold back since the deceased cannot hurt you in any way.

2. ***A photo or a memory item:***

    If talking to an empty chair doesn't appeal to you, look at a photograph of the deceased and try to capture that image in your mind. Holding on to that image, talk to him or her in the same way.

3. *Walking in the woods:*

Some people can do much of the talking by walking alone in nature. Select a place where you can have privacy. Rather than thinking about it, talk normally as if you were physically with the deceased. Remember that thinking and physically voicing your thoughts are two different processes. Thinking alone can retain your negative energy. Talking can, however, release some of the bottled up energy residing in you.

SOME OUTRAGEOUS GESTURES THAT MAY RELIEVE ANGER:

1. *A dead fly:*

Someone told me to imagine a dead fly in my palm and blow it off! Maybe the deceased caused you that kind of pain. Blowing that dead fly off of your palm in one big and forceful blow might make the stress feel less. No harm done!

2. *Bubbles:*

Save sheets of bubble wrapping (plastic wrapping for packaging) and line them up on the floor. Hop on the bubbles and pop them until you have no more energy left. Yell at the deceased while you're doing this. Swing your arms around. Be creative!

3. *Whispering:*

Take a deep breath through your nose and say, "I'm mad at you!" or whatever you want to say in the strongest whisper you can voice. Repeat it until you are tired of doing it.

4. **Exercising:**

   Combine some exercises while you're doing step 3. For example, nod your head forward three times after you say, "I'm mad at you."

5. **Piano:**

   If you have a piano nearby, create an outrageous composition that displays your emotions. You do not need to know how to play the piano. All you need are two hands (or feet).

6. **Opera:**

   Take a radio into the bathroom (avoid being electrocuted), find a classical station that is playing opera, and harmonize while taking a shower. Make sure you use your diaphragm the way Pavarotti sings.

7. **Food:**

   If you're on a diet, go off the diet for one day. Eat all the ice cream and brownies you want without feeling guilty. You have my permission!

8. **Planting a tree:**

   Dig a big hole and plant a tree. Call it your "Anger Tree." Talk to it everyday and watch it transform into a gorgeous tree. Even if you don't have a green thumb and it dies, you would have had a living body that listened to all your concerns.

9. **You're ok:**

   Shout all the negative thoughts that are bottled up in you and at the end, pat yourself on both shoulders and say, "You're OK," or "I forgive you."

A single event can awaken within us
A stranger totally unknown to us.
To live is to be slowly born.

ANTOINE DE SAINT-EXUPÉRY

7. Forgiving

FORGIVE AND FORGET!

The most difficult and the most needed task in life seems to be the act of forgiving. Yet, we hardly know what forgiveness means or how we achieve it. How often do we hear people say "You must forgive and forget" when facing anger and resentment? Some even expect God to do this task for us. Whether God forgives or not, on this earth, in our life, forgiveness still remains our responsibility. Recently, I asked myself the following questions: Should we really forget in order to forgive? Do "forgiving" and "forgetting" have a sequential or causal relationship? Do we forgive in layers as we peel onions? Do we forgive once? Or do we forgive multiple times in our lifetime over the same event?

Your husband runs off with a younger woman.
"You've got to forgive and forget."
Your friends have died in a war.
"You've got to forgive and forget."
Your child was abused by a neighbor.
"You've got to forgive and forget."
Your contractor ran away with your money.
"You've got to forgive and forget."
Your last words to your father were that you hated him.
"You've got to forgive and forget."

The irony is that our society encourages us to *remember,* not to forget. In our years of schooling, we are taught to remember, not to forget. The higher the SAT score, the better college choices we have. The brighter we are, the better jobs we may get. Are there rewards for forgetting? Furthermore, *remembering* seems to be

75   *Talking, Writing, Doing*

easier when there are emotions attached. Those of us who have gone through traumatic experiences remember every word and every action. When we are "wronged" by someone, our remembering goes into full force, supported by our strong emotions. Thus, although we can academically or spiritually say to ourselves, "forgive and forget," the act of forgetting is more difficult than we think.

Forgetting, however, is also a natural way of letting us find a balance in a traumatic situation. When we have wronged someone and we have no internal resource to face it, we may choose to forget the past and even rewrite the past to move on. In a divorce, it's common to find ex-spouses with two totally different realities of what happened. One reality was based on a keen remembrance of what happened because it hurt. The other reality may be based on a real need to escape from the realization that he or she has hurt someone. So *remembering* and *forgetting* play a big role in how we deal with life.

When we force ourselves to forget in order to forgive, however, aren't we taking an unnatural path? We are remembering because we hurt and because we sense anger from the injustice or unfairness we faced. Our emotions help us remember those facts. How can we deny those feelings by simply saying, "Forget about it"? The law of physics on the conservation of energy applies here. We can recycle energy but cannot destroy it. We cannot simply wipe away our feelings and say, "I forget!" We can, however, accept our feelings and view them from a different perspective, which we will discuss later in this section.

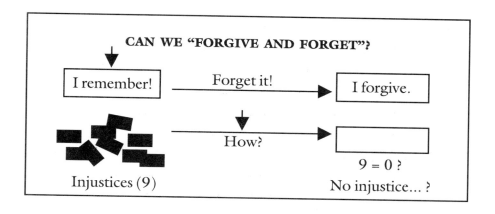

FORGIVING MORE THAN ONCE

The act of saying "I forgive you" sometimes has little effect on our feelings. When we delete a computer file, we click on "delete," and it will most likely be put in the computer's "trash can." We have not deleted it in reality until we empty the trash can. Similarly, we can say "I forgive you" mentally, but our negative feelings may be living persistently in our "trash can." Those feelings may resurrect themselves and haunt us again. Unfortunately, it is not as easy to empty our trash can full of old feelings as we can with the computer files.

I have seen this in my own life. Since I had little direct communication with my ex-husband, "forgiving" was really done with two voices within me, one saying, "I hurt," and the other saying, "Love him in spite of it." While I believe I have "forgiven" him for the past, a new situation reminding me of the past can bring a resurgence of the old feelings. In divorce, as with the anniversaries of death, there is a cycle we seem to go through. As our children grow and go through their own marriages and child-rearing, we relive the memory of the good and bad experiences shared with our ex-spouses. Thus, the old feelings of abandonment can return, however controlled those feelings may be after many years. After spending some time facing our renewed anger, we would go through the process of "forgiving" again! What we have not accepted is that we may forgive many times over the same problem in our lifetime.

Because we live in a complex society where we must face the people who wronged us in the past in new situations, we keep on working on our feelings and forgiveness. It is similar to how we form a pot from wet clay. We think we have a finished product, but one jerky stroke may force it to tumble down on the pottery wheel. We start all over. Hopefully, each time, we find it easier to build it back up, as our skills of forgiving improve in time. Some of our pots remain unfinished before our life ends. That is OK, too. We are not perfect, even in our act of forgiveness. What counts is that we keep on trying. As the Japanese proverb says, "Fall seven times, rise eight times."

FORGIVING THE DECEASED

If human beings only left behind memories of good deeds, mourning would be a much easier process. It would still hurt, of course, but it is easier to conclude a relationship that was full of good memories than it is to deal with an unfinished, dysfunctional or abusive relationship. Mourning in the latter case is often ignored.

Some mourners deny the need to mourn a conflicted, ambivalent relationship they had with the deceased. It seems that death should end the past and bring a sense of relief. What they don't realize is that deceased do not take the survivors' memories with them when they die. The unresolved problems continue to remain unresolved in the survivors' minds.

Therese Rando discusses the need for mourning a negative relationship in her book, *Treatment of Complicated Mourning* (1993, Research Press). The following four issues are from the eight she raises on this topic (pp. 476-7).

◆ Mourning the death of an abusive individual does not invalidate the abuse, lessen the culpability of the perpetrator or victimization of the mourner, or mean the mourner wishes the deceased were alive to resume the relationship.

◆ Negative ties can bind just as strongly as positive ones, with the degree of bonding being determined by the strength of attachment, not its characteristics. Characteristics of the bond determine only the quality of the attachment.

◆ All ties, whether positive or negative, must be relinquished. This demands mourning.

◆ Much of the mourning that must take place after the death of an abuser focuses on mourning for what that abuser has taken away from the mourner (e.g., innocence, autonomy, a happy childhood, trust.)

In other words, mourning the deceased who robbed you of certain rights does not mean that you are condoning what he or she did. You are simply breaking the negative bond you had with the deceased. It's as if an invisible rope held you in bondage to this individual in life, and although the death removed him or her physically from your life, the rope is still there. Mourning simply means relinquishing those bonds, or ties. Forgiveness, perhaps, is the critical part of relinquishing ties to that relationship.

There are many books written on life-after-death experiences, whether it is through hypnosis or reports from those who have been revived after being "dead." One common element that these reports share is that at death, one is exposed to the truth. The soul recalls all deeds committed in life, good and bad. Whether you believe this concept or not, wouldn't it be reassuring to think that the deceased may recognize the pain he or she caused and ask for forgiveness? You have nothing to lose from thinking this way!

Whatever your religious beliefs may be, the fact is that sometimes the words of forgiveness do not remove those invisible bonds left by the deceased. As old habits are hard to break, old bonds, as negative as they may be, are also hard to break. Since we naturally relate well to concrete gestures, a mourning ceremony involving (1) making a list of complaints, (2) having a two-way conversation with the deceased, and (3) forgiving each deed, can give you some sense of relief. The trick is to "exorcize" your mind from the clutter left behind by the painful, unfinished, dysfunctional relationship. A grief counselor can help you to let this part of your past "expire." The bad deeds remain bad deeds. No memory is erased. Yet, you will not be bound to the memory of these deeds.

MANIPULATING OUR VIEWS

Do you remember playing with a kaleidoscope? You shake it, and when you stop, your view through the opening shows a new design formed by the colorful speckles. With a slight movement, another design forms from the same speckles. We are not that simple, but the kaleidoscope resembles the way we work with our facts and feelings. We get angry, and we shake up our speckles in us until we form a design. We stay there sometimes unshaken, locked into that design. Then some sudden movement, perhaps a slight shift in our view, changes the design entirely. The design can go from hot, flashy speckles to soothing, subdued speckles in seconds!

Does the act of transforming our resentment to peace, from anger to compassion, happen as easily as the kaleidoscope analogy? Probably not. However, the switch may not be as difficult as we believe. How often have we struggled so hard to say "I'm sorry," and found ourselves relieved after having said it, wondering why it took so long? The design in our head is totally rearranged, and gone are the angry, red speckles! Do we remember the old design? Yes! Do we enjoy the new, peaceful design? Maybe. If we had stayed in the original, angry design and repeatedly told ourselves to forget it all, would the design change by itself? Probably not. It takes a change in how we view the problem, and only we have that control. We control our kaleidoscope.

If we *allow* ourselves to forgive without forgetting, then the task of going from pure anger to somewhat forgiving thoughts may be easier. You can forgive while exercising the right to remember. There is no need to force yourself to forget what happened. Here are some practical ways of doing it. It's all about switching your lenses or changing the degree of magnification.

1. *Be glad you're not living his (her) life.*

   This is one time you can allow yourself to feel a sense of "superiority" for the sake of letting go of your anger. Let's say that your view includes fairness and compassion for others, as opposed to the view of another, based on lies and cheating. You are operating on different planes, each having a value system. If you can be a bit arrogant and say that you have been *blessed* with more ability to act with the love for others while the person you resent cannot feel that love, you might find it easier to let go of your anger. Tell yourself, "It's too bad his (her) view is limited." "I'm glad I don't have to carry his (her) burden." "We go by different rules."

2. *Replenish your compassion.*

   I recently went through a terribly unfair and hurtful arbitration case with the state's consumer board. The board supported the judge's biased opinion without attention given to the documented evidence. The contractor, with his lawyer, walked away with not one blemish on his record, after presenting fiction and lies. I learned later that I would have easily won in court. By going through the consumer board, I lost my right to use the small claim's court to be reimbursed. Was I angry? Yes! Could I "forgive and forget?"

No! After several weeks, I am still fuming over how such injustice could occur. I am, however, rising above the situation by (1) feeling peaceful that my conscience is clear, leaving the contractor to wrestle with his conscience; and (2) turning this sense of anger over the system's injustice to educate others by sharing my experience and newly found knowledge. By the time I write an article on this issue, I will be able to write it with humor and with a goal to help others. If you are willing to look at your situation in this manner, give yourself time. You have the right to feel anger after being wronged. However, living with that anger damages your life, not the person who wronged you. It can be seen later with humor or with a real desire to help others based on your experience. Forgiveness, thus, can mean turning your anger into a positive energy source within you.

3. **Ask: "Will this be important if I knew today was the last day of my life?"**

This question, to me, is the most effective question in that most problems seem insignificant when we value our life with death in mind. If the answer is "yes," then you have a goal that needs to be worked out immediately. Perhaps it's something you cannot ignore. Some very important social changes came from a sense of commitment to fight against injustice. Most problems, however, lose their intensity when viewed with this question.

Give yourself permission:

    1. To have anger.

    2. To remember what happened.

Then ask yourself:

    1. Is my anger really important in my life?

    2. Am I having a good time?

    3. Have I stayed here long enough?

    4. When shall I move on?

Then get ready to switch from anger to compassion.

Tell yourself:

    1. I'm glad I'm not in his (her) place!

    2. It's not important enough in the scheme of life.

    3. I'm converting my anger to compassion.

    4. I'm moving on.

ON FORGIVING:

*Who are on my "black list" of people who have betrayed me?
(You may include family, friends, co-workers, contractors,
politicians, etc!)*

_____

_____

_____

_____

_____

_____

_____

_____

Pick one to work on:

_____

*Describe how you feel (the red speckles) about your view seen
through the kaleidoscope.*

_____

_____

_____

_____

_____

_____

Are you set in this view? Is your kaleidoscope immobile, frozen to this design?

_____

_____

_____

_____

How long have I been frozen with this view?

_____

_____

_____

_____

Are you having a great time with your eyes set on this design? Describe your energy level.

_____

_____

_____

_____

Now tell yourself the following:

SELF-TALK:
1. I'm glad I'm not in his (her) place!
2. It's OK to be angry for a while.
3. Is this anger really important to my life?
4. I'm changing my kaleidoscope design.
5. I don't have to forget what happened.

Directions:

As a sign of having switched your design, do something symbolic so that your thoughts become your action. For example, you can write a positive letter to the person, whether you send it or not, or put a flower in a vase and say it's for you, whether you show it to her (him) or not.

My new design is:

_____

_____

_____

_____

_____

MY VIEW THROUGH THE KALEIDOSCOPE

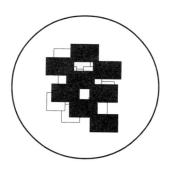 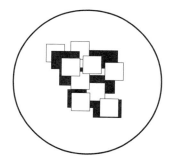

Sometimes I go about pitying myself,
and all the time
I am being carried
on great wings across the sky.

Ojibway Saying

8. *Your Creativity*

A traumatic event can certainly dry up your stored energy. It is, however, a time when you may also discover creativity that you didn't recognize in you before. Think of Beethoven who composed such complex and wonderful symphonies when he was going deaf.

In my case, it was music, poetry and gardening. I sang Gounod's *Ave Maria* during my first year of mourning, remembering how my mother used to accompany me on the piano. After a few weeks, I noticed that my dog, Rockie, was always near the piano bench when *Ave Maria* was being played. Soon, all I had to say was *"Ave Maria!"* and he would walk over to the piano. Rockie and I shared a very special, daily routine of singing to my mother. I also remembered something funny that my mother and I shared. I once sang a Japanese song at a recital, and I forgot all the lyrics. My mother's jaw dropped in a state of shock when I continued to sing in gibberish after deciding that no one would know since there were no Japanese in the audience. Her comment afterward was her usual, "Oh, You-u-u!" with a big smile saying "You messed up again!" Years later, I was singing all the right words for her. Thus music was a form of relief for me, as were writing and gardening.

Be willing to try new areas of interest. My mother's love for flowers somehow became my new source of joy. Seeing colorful flowers reminded me of the joy she saw in new blooms, especially the rare flowers that only she could grow indoors. What a great way to honor the person you loved so much — by continuing the legacy of your loved one's interest. Of course, know your limits to avoid further stress! I never did attempt to do the craft work she was able to do. I knew my fingers would be full of needle marks, and the stitches never would have been straight like hers. I would have developed ulcers from replicating her work! But in music and in flowers, I found a positive path from sorrow to happy memories. Somehow, I was going from missing her to sensing her presence.

Keep a green tree in your heart
and perhaps a singing bird
will come.

CHINESE PROVERB

WHAT ARE YOUR CREATIVE TOOLS?

_____

_____

_____

_____

_____

_____

CREATIVITY - DETAILS

My old creativity tools that would soothe my feelings:

New areas of interest:

9. Memorializing

Funerals and memorial services have a place in our lives. Some believe that they are strictly to honor the deceased. Some believe they are traditions of the past. I actually had believed both until my mother died. What is often not understood is that they are just as much for the survivors as they are for the deceased. They are social and spiritual events where friends and family come together to express love, share their grief and offer support. It also gives everyone a chance to feel a sense of closure.

This opportunity to express the loss may not be available for you; for example, losses involving a death of a newborn where there was no funeral, death of a pet, a miscarriage, divorce, etc. There may be other losses not recognized by society, such as the death of a lover outside of the marriage (putting all moral judgment aside here) or catastrophic deaths that friends and family find difficult to discuss. In such cases, you can still create your own way of memorializing the life of the person (or a pet) who died.

It may be in forms of drawing, writing or something as philanthropic as taking on a cause. Darlene Armacost recently lost her teenage daughter to cancer. She is dedicating her time to develop and support the *Ashley Foundation,* a newly formed foundation for adolescents with terminal illnesses.

SOME IDEAS ON MEMORIALIZING:

◆ *Planting a tree*
Caution: Trees and flowers can die, so be prepared for that possibility. My pink dogwood tree planted in my mother's honor has white flowers and almost died during the first year.

- *Framing pictures or making collages*
  This is a very rewarding experience and not costly. Small photographs can create wonderful reminders of the loved ones.

- *Writing poems and keeping a diary*
  Poems do not need to rhyme. Enjoy experimenting with the sound of words.

- *Sketching and drawing*

- *Learning a new piece of music or writing a song*

- *Choosing a charity of choice (one that your beloved respected) and actively volunteering*

- *Making a memory box and placing special items inside*

- *Making a special album or a scrapbook*

- *Picking a special day to invite friends or family to share the positive memories*

- *Making special "care packages of memories" to those who loved him or her*
  (If you have a lot of special memory items, rather than hogging them, share them with friends. You will get a lot of joy from extending the circle of love this way.)

- *Dining out with friends and tell them, "It's on _____(the deceased)."*

- *Placing flowers and special rocks at the place of the accident*

- *Committing to do something in that person's honor*
  (This goal can be kept private.)

◆ Making a phone call to a friend or a neighbor who just lost their loved one and do it in the memory of your loved one

◆ Submitting a statement of love in the obituary section of the local newspaper

◆ Contributing to an organization that gave pleasure to your loved one

Directions: See if you can think of additional possibilities on your own. Be creative!

1. _____

2. _____

3. _____

SPACE FOR CREATIVE THOUGHTS

MEMORIALIZING

What:

_____

_____

_____

_____

When:

_____

_____

_____

_____

How:

_____

_____

_____

_____

With Whom:

_____

_____

_____

_____

10. Holidays

Holidays and anniversary dates can be difficult for you. Special dates your loved one could have shared with you had he or she lived will bring out emotions in you. As long as you live, if you had a special relationship with this person, there will be moments when you will think, "I wish he (she) were here." It's natural. On anniversaries of special days that we used to share with our loved one, we can prevent our feelings of sorrow by mentally preparing ahead of time and making concrete plans.

SOME SUGGESTIONS:

1. *Make a list of dates:*
   Keep a list of dates that you and your loved one shared, and be prepared that those dates can be difficult for you.

2. *Do things differently:*
   On your first anniversary dates, such as your wedding anniversary, your or your loved one's birthday, Mother's Day, etc., you might want to do something different. For example, on the first Mother's Day without your mother, you can invite an aunt or a friend without children and treat her to dinner.

3. *Say "no":*
   Practice your right to decline an invitation. If spending Thanksgiving with your family is too big a step for you, talk to your family and do something different, such as volunteering at a homeless shelter. Before deciding to be alone on a special day, ask yourself if that is what you really want, or if you simply need a change of pace.

4. **Communicate openly:**
   Tell your family and friends exactly how you are feeling, and ask them to be patient. You have the right to say that you appreciate their plans but you are apprehensive about having a big holiday celebration.

5. **Be with supportive people:**
   Know who can provide you with comforting words when sadness overwhelms you. Have their phone numbers ready.

6. **Find time to center yourself:**
   Walk in the park. Read quietly. Listen to the rain. Let the miracle of silence soothe your feelings.

7. **There is no time limit to grief:**
   Give yourself the right to have feelings years after the loss. Time does not dictate when grief ends.

Don't let people drive you crazy
when you know it's in walking distance.

AUTHOR UNKNOWN

DATES TO REMEMBER - MINE

Date	Event	Celebrate by doing . . .	Celebrate with . . .

Talking, Writing, Doing

DATES TO REMEMBER - OTHERS
(Reaching out . . .)

Date	Event	Celebrate by doing . . .	Celebrate with . . .

11. Time for a Change

At times of adversity, we often find a new meaning in life. Our thoughts may seem cluttered, but we may be closer to knowing ourselves. It's time when we make apologies that seemed impossible to make. It's also time to hug and feel the love of others in ways we never could do before. Why not take this opportunity to make a new goal for the future?

A NEW GOAL:

Define:

_____

_____

_____

_____

_____

Time frame:

_____

_____

_____

_____

Steps toward achievement:

_____

_____

_____

Symbolism:
(What would you use to remind
yourself of this goal that you set?)

_____

_____

_____

_____

_____

_____

Rewards:

_____

_____

_____

_____

_____

There is a soul force in the universe,
which, if we permit it,
will flow through us and produce
miraculous results.

MAHATMA GHANDI

When you get to the end of your rope,
tie a knot and hang on.

FRANKLIN D. ROOSEVELT

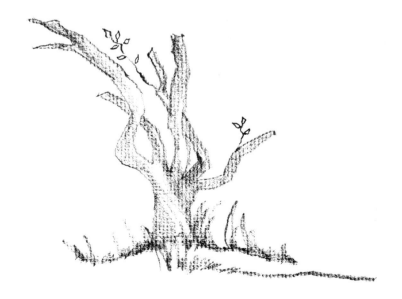

Section III:

$\mathcal{U}$NDERSTANDING

Grief experiences:

HISTORICAL ASPECTS

PHASES AND TASKS OF GRIEF

TYPES OF DEATH

SYMPTOMS

CULTURAL ASPECTS

Human grief is universal and is part of life.
Yet its individual uniqueness makes it
difficult to comprehend another's grief or
to express one's own grief to others.
Understanding the nature of grief enables
us to help ourselves and others with more
openness and patience.

*Joy and pain
can live in the same house.
Neither should deny the other.*

TAN NENG

WHAT THIS SECTION COVERS

Since Elisabeth Kübler-Ross published her book, *On Death and Dying*, many others have expanded upon what she wrote. This section will (1) summarize the historical aspects of human grief; (2) introduce some of the current thinking in the area of grief; and (3) list symptoms that are within the natural course of grief and others that may require counseling.

1. *Historical Aspects on Death and Grief*

2. *The Grief Process*

3. *Grief Tasks*

4. *Types of Death*

5. *Difficult Death*

6. *Grief Styles*

7. *Awareness Levels*

8. *Grief Symptoms*

9. *Complicated Grief*

10. *Disenfranchised Grief*

11. *Children and Grief*

12. *Elderly and Grief*

13. *Pet Loss*

14. *Multicultural Interest*

A Griever in Us

There are things . . .

>*. . . that we don't want to see*
>>*but we open our eyes*

>*. . . that we don't want to feel*
>>*but we struggle to connect*

>*. . . that we don't want to lose*
>>*but we learn to live without*

>*. . . that we don't want to believe*
>>*but we undress our soul*

So that we will feel that Love again

KEI GILBERT

1. Historical Aspects of Death and Grief

Have we always viewed death in the same way throughout history? Has the concept of heaven and hell or eternal life always possessed the minds of men and women? Did we always respect the body of the deceased in the manner we do now? Here is a brief summary of how the Western World changed the ways we view death and dying.

EGYPTIAN DAYS

Ancient Egyptian kings were mummified to make sure that the body stayed alive after death until the parts of their soul would return and were united to protect the people. Men's souls consisted of three parts — Ba (similar to personality), Ka (the life force), and Akh (formed when Ba and Ka unite). At birth, Ba and Ka were together, and at death, they were again separate. After death, Ka stayed with the body. Ba went to the underworld to face challenges and was eventually united with Ka to form Akh, which in turn protected the king and his people.

UP TO THE MIDDLE AGES

Men and women didn't live long, and death was everywhere. Children were not inoculated against childhood illnesses, so they often died as infants. Death was part of life then. The bodies were allowed to rot, and the bones were placed in a place called ossuaries. The dead, in other words, were viewed openly, and the everyday events took place without any revulsion to the sight or the odor. People sold goods and ate food in the same place where the bodies were being dried. Life was difficult but simple.

THE PLAGUE

Brought on by fleas, the Black Plague infected many, and the rich fled the area or died from the plague. The economic and social structures thus changed, and nouveau riche (the middle class) entered the scene of religious rites. The simple outlook on life was tainted by the devastating and horrifying nature of the plague.

DEATH OF SELF

In the 16th century, with the advent of science and medical dissection, men became more interested in the human body itself. By the 18th century, most bodies were placed in individual graves in cemeteries which were often located outside of town.

Death also became the scene of a struggle between the devil and God. The clergy were called to deathbeds to assist in this battle with the devil. The paintings of this era often show this conflict taking place above the dying person. The fear of being taken by the devil and the question of heaven and hell became a big part of the dying scene.

THE DEATH OF OTHERS

The 18th century philosopher Rousseau talked about man's relationship and communion with nature. Men were born equal in the laws of nature. The modern concept of grief of an individual was born during this period. Death left one with a sense of longing, and a hope for a reunion in the future. The rise of the Protestant movement brought longing and fear. In Calvinism and Puritanism, where only the "chosen ones" went to heaven after death, men and women faced not only sorrow but fear as well. Grief thus included missing the loved one, wishing to be reunited, but not knowing if they would.

THE DISTANT DEATH

Embalming was done during the U.S. Civil War to prevent the soldiers' bodies from decaying as they were shipped home. After the war, the funeral directors took on the role of embalming. The insurance business and the funeral directors became focused on managing death, and men and women became more and more distant from being connected with the dead. You lived; you died.

THE 21ST CENTURY CONCEPT OF DEATH

The elderly are often placed in nursing homes, where the dying process may not be seen closely by the family. Young children have fewer opportunities to interact with the elderly, and many grow up feeling that growing old is not beautiful. Deaths portrayed in the movies are often related to violence, which children may not distinguish from fiction. Thus the younger generation has difficulty relating to death that enters their world. Funerals have lost meaning to some, and there is a trend to rethink the ways we mourn. What does remain with us, though, is the universality of grief itself. Whether we are wealthy or poor, educated or not, healthy or sick, tender or rough, we all experience grief to some extent. Death is not escapable.

The living are now encouraged to plan their funerals or make known their wishes on how to die, as in creating a Living Will. The Internet is also changing our understanding of grief, since a quick search can locate a multitude of sites related to human loss and pet loss. Internet memorializing is becoming common these days. Perhaps the future will bring a blend of creative and traditional styles of mourning for a loss that is nevertheless painful.

For further information on the historical aspects on the death and dying, read *Western Attitudes toward Death* by Philippe Ariès. Aries discusses the historical aspects of man's view of death from the middle ages to the present in four periods: 1) Tamed death, 2) One's own death, 3) Thy death, and 4) Forbidden death.

How far you go in life depends on
your being tender with the young,
compassionate with the aged,
sympathetic with the striving
and tolerant of the weak and strong.

Because someday in your life,
you will have been all of these.

GEORGE WASHINGTON CARVER

Ariès, Philippe. (1975). *Western Attitudes toward Death.* Baltimore, Maryland: The Johns Hopkins University Press.

2. The Grief Process

In 1969, Elisabeth Kübler-Ross wrote *On Death and Dying*, which became the focal point in our study on the process of dying. Her concept was that there were five stages involved in accepting death: (1) denial and isolation, (2) anger, (3) bargaining, (4) depression, and (5) acceptance. Initially, it was believed that these stages were sequential and linear. With the widened understanding of death and dying, others have expanded her concept or contradicted some of the elements. The prevailing belief is that those steps are not necessarily sequential, and that they may occur concurrently or are skipped.

PHASES OF GRIEF

The following three steps are commonly accepted by psychologists on how we deal with a significant loss:

(1) Shock and denial

We may experience a sense of shock and deny, consciously or not, that the loss occurred. This time frame involves a lot of emotional expressions.

(2) Adjustment to the loss

After the dust settles, we begin to accept that the loss occurred. This time frame involves much effort to take concrete steps in letting go of our ties.

(3) Reinvestment in the future

A quilt can be patched back together. As in my kimono poem, life can be washed and sewn back together. A broken dish can be glued back together. This time frame involves making a whole of the parts, again becoming something useful. We move on with life, while we may continue to shelter some of the grief or memories in our thoughts.

If you look around and view the people around you, you will see that no two people go through these three steps in the same way. Some stay in denial for many years, while others move on to recreate their new future right away. Most of us go from denial to reality like a yo-yo for a while. At first, we're devastated by the loss and spend time thinking that it's just a bad dream. Then slowly, our denial is chipped away as time reinforces the new reality of the loss. Again, with steps 2 and 3, we move at our own pace, some making a great strive toward a positive change, while others struggle and choose to stay behind.

The second step, "adjustment to the loss," is where we can do a lot of work toward finding closure to the loss by expressing our emotions and memorializing through our personal, creative ways. (See Section II.)

How or how long we grieve is affected by many variables. Here are some of the factors which may affect the way we grieve:

◆ *Age*

◆ *Intelligence*

◆ *Mental health*

◆ *Maturity level*

◆ *Established coping patterns*

◆ *Past history of losses*

◆ *Unresolved grief from the past losses*

◆ *Accumulated stress; other sources of stress*

◆ *Social, cultural, ethnic, religious and philosophical background*

◆ *Sex-role conditioning*

◆ *Relationship with the deceased:*

    - type (sibling, parent, friend, etc.)

    - quality

    - length

    - intensity

*Each small task of every day life
is part of the total harmony
of the Universe.*

SAINT TÉRÈSE OF LISIEUX

3. Grief Tasks

A SPIDER WEB

The most amazing miracle of life is that a spider can recreate its intricate web in a short time after someone or something destroys it. When we lose any part of our web, our life's work, we seem to move in slow motion for a while, unable to recreate it as the spiders can. Are we so different from the spiders, though? We strive to weave our life just as a spider busily weaves its web, from the center to the outer rim, in and out, and from side to side. If the web is destroyed, we, like the spider, still have the ability to make another web. The threads are ready to be used any time we decide to move on in life again. Why would it be different for us in how we learn to cope with a loss? When our web collapses, we continue to make another web. The difference is that the spiders don't question the "why's." They rely on the "how's." We must also focus on our learning tools to deal with our losses.

OUR CRUTCHES

J. William Worden, a psychologist, describes the grief tasks as the following four tasks:

1. Accept the reality of the loss.
2. Experience the pain.
3. Learn to adjust to the altered world.
4. Reinvest in life and living.

Most of the human process of learning involves tools and hard work. A baby uses a walker to learn to stay upright. A child uses training wheels to learn to ride a bike. A beginning snow skier uses short skis to learn to makes turns. If you break a leg, you walk with the help of crutches. With grief, we can also use crutches to move from denial to acceptance of the loss. Our crutches enable us to deal with the heaviness of grief. They are helpful as long as we don't allow our crutches to become our legs. What then are the crutches we use in grief?

Assuming that our path from the initial shock to reinventing the future is a path we must walk after the loss, let's explore what "crutches" we can use to speed up our learning. We learn a new skill by evaluating what we *see, say, touch, hear,* and *do.* We also learn from what we see others *see, say, touch, hear,* and *do.* The crutches we use during grief are the tasks that use those five modes of learning.

You have done Section II of this workbook, which includes many of the tasks that involve these five modes of learning. They are your crutches. Writing to yourself in a diary *(talking)* unloads your emotions. Reading *(seeing)* inspirational or spiritual books uplifts you. Listening *(hearing)* to soothing music leads you toward tranquility. Devoting your time to a new cause or planting a tree *(doing)* allows you to take one step away from anger, chaos and depression. Browsing through *(touching)* memory items of your loved one helps you build a bridge from grief to memory. They are all crutches that you may lean on to adjust to a new way of walking.

LETTING GO

Letting go is often a slow process. The steps toward letting go can happen through our conscious effort, spontaneously or sometimes slowly and subconsciously. We wonder, though, if we ever finish grieving. Sigmund Freud believed otherwise. He believed that the ties to the old relationship needed to be cut, but that the task was never completed. John Bowlby believed that instead of cutting ties, we replaced previous attachment with another attachment. Letting go also does not mean forgetting the loved one. It simply means turning sorrow into positive memories and storing them in a place. We can then readily retrieve them as needed. The common understanding among the psychologists is that grief expends much energy. As infants use all their strength to take that one big step as they learn to walk, we, too, use our energy to work with our grief. Kübler-Ross believed that in every stage of grief, there is, however, a sense of hope. Hope and renewal are at the heart of our existence, as in all human experiences.

Corr, Charles A., Nabe, Clyde M. and Corr, Donna M. (1997). *Death & Dying, Life & Living*. New York, NY: Brooks/Cole Publishing.

Kübler-Ross, Elisabeth. (1969). *On Death and Dying.* New York, NY: MacMillan Publishing.

Worden, J. William. (1991) *Grief Counseling & Grief Therapy*. New York, NY: Springer Publishing.

*It is possible to provide security
against all ills,
but as far as death
is concerned,
we men live in a city
without walls.*

EPICURUS

4. Types of Death

Many of us with little exposure to death assume that we all grieve in the same way over each death, or each significant loss of someone special in our life. The truth is that although death is one common denominator we all share in our life, each death comes disguised in varied ways, some more difficult than others for both the dying and those left behind. The following describes types of death.

APPROPRIATE DEATH:
Death that occurs in the manner the dying would have wished, reducing conflict for the survivors, allowing the continuity of a meaningful relationship

TIMELY DEATH:
Death that occurs at an appropriate time, such as in old age, after having had a full and productive life

SUDDEN DEATH:
Death that comes unexpected

TRAUMATIC DEATH:
Death that is unnatural and dramatic; e.g., suicide, homicide, and other violent sources of death

PROLONGED DEATH:
Death that comes after a lengthy illness, often with physical and/or mental debilitation; e.g., Alzheimer's, Lou Gehrig's disease (ALS)

Understanding

PREMATURE DEATH:
Death that occurs prematurely according to our calendar of life's events; e.g., sudden-infant-death syndrome (SIDS), death of a child, death of a young pet.

Two people grieving over a loss — one of a 95-year-old grandfather who had a great career and a blessed family life and another of a six-week-old infant due to SIDS — may have a drastic difference in the way they grieve. In one, the survivor can celebrate the long and completed life, and in the other, the survivor questions the timing of the event and grieves for the future they are not able to share.

Death may also fall into several types; for example, a prolonged death may have ended with a traumatic and sudden twist. A suicide of a young child is not only a sudden and traumatic death, but it is also a shortened life.

In helping someone in grief, we must practice empathy without making assumptions on another's grief. There is a Chinese proverb that says, "Only he who has traveled the road knows where the holes are deep." Since our paths in life may cross but are never identical, we can only imagine the depth of the holes our friends face. The best we can do is to simply offer a hand along the way. Grief is our individual reaction to the holes we face.

5. Difficult Death

By classifying some deaths as "difficult," it is not to say that other deaths are not difficult. However, we will discuss further the last four types of death listed in the previous section: 1) sudden death, 2) traumatic death, 3) prolonged death, and 4) shortened life.

SUDDEN DEATH:

Your loved one dies from complications from surgery where he or she was expected to recover or be discharged from the hospital. A minor illness suddenly takes a turn. A heart attack. A stroke. A fatal car accident. A random shooting. There was no opportunity to prepare for the loss. The survivor will most likely face a pronounced state of shock and a sense of denial.

TRAUMATIC DEATH:

Often a sudden death as well, a traumatic death leaves a strong impression on the actual or imagined images of the way the loved one died. The images can haunt the survivors for a long time; however, with the right expression of grief, these troubling images can fade in time.

PROLONGED DEATH:

With improved health care, unfortunately, more people die slowly. The life of a dying person afflicted with long-term and often painful or debilitating illness is not easy. It is especially difficult for the caretakers, whether they are nearby or far away. The caretakers grieve as they watch their loved ones deteriorate. When death actually occurs, they are often exhausted and may feel guilty that death did not bring sadness but a sense of relief. Unlike sudden death, much grieving is done before death takes place. Some may question their faith, asking why a benevolent God would allow someone to suffer for so long.

SHORTENED LIFE:

A death of a child, especially an infant or a young one, is difficult, particularly for the parents. They question why the unfinished life still full of promises was cut short abruptly. It is difficult in that every year that the parents are alive, they think of what their child would have done or become. An infant who died lives, at least in the minds and hearts of parents. The child grows older every year as do other children with every birthday. With infant deaths, it is important to memorialize more openly and personally because it is often easily forgotten by others. Unlike an 80-year-old friend or a parent with whom they have a history of shared memory, an infant's short life has less impact on others outside of the immediate family. A simple act of candle-lighting on the anniversary of the infant's death can give an outlet for the parents to grieve without suppressing their feelings.

6. The Grief Styles

This segment is contributed by Terry Martin, Ph.D., the author of the book, *Men Don't Cry . . . Women Do.*

GENDER AND GRIEF:
Many people assume that, with all of the noticeable differences between men and women, they must grieve differently as well. There are studies that highlight how women and men differ in their grief. In short, men make a faster social recovery from loss (go back to work, resume previous activities, begin to date), while women show a stronger emotional recovery, especially one year after the loss. There are also studies that could not find any significant differences between how men and women grieve. For a brief review of the most relevant studies, read Chapter 7 of the book, *Men Don't Cry . . . Women Do.*

TWO STYLES OF GRIEF:
While gender and gender roles influence an individual's grief, they may not necessarily determine how that person will grieve. Martin and Doka explore, in their book, a process of grief beyond the styles associated with gender. Their concept centers around a process of seeing grief as a continuum between two styles of grieving: instrumental and intuitive.

TWO GRIEF STYLES

(A continuum)

Instrumental Grief ◄ ┄┄┄┄┄┄┄┄┄┄┄┄┄┄┄ ► Intuitive Grief

Instrumental grievers tend to:
1. Experience their grief as more thinking than feeling
2. Show their grief more as action, such as telling stories about the person or administering a scholarship fund or building some memorial to the deceased
3. Avoid seeking help with grief

Intuitive grievers tend to:
1. Experience their grief as very intense feelings
2. Show their feelings openly and often
3. Seek out others with whom they can share their feelings

Most people are a blend of the two styles, with one being slightly more dominant than the other. Take a look at how you have grieved for your loved ones to see if you have a preferred style in the continuum between instrumental and intuitive styles.

Remember that you are much more than your gender. Your personality, family, upbringing, and culture may also affect how you grieve.

Martin, Terry L. and Doka, Kenneth J. (2000). *Men Don't Cry . . . Women Do.* Philadelphia, PA: Brunner/Mazel.

7. Awareness Levels

Facing grief over an approaching death or a recent death, we operate out of our personal set of rules defined by our emotions, molded by cultural and societal expectations. At a funeral, we might hear someone whispering, "Poor John, his eyes are red from crying," or "Why doesn't Susan look sad?" We might even hear criticism on how someone is still grieving for his or her loved one beyond a few years. "Peter needs to move on!" someone mutters. Another whispers, "Can you believe Ann remarried after only a few weeks?"

We look at death or a loss through shades tinted with personal beliefs and experiences. Because we have preferences in the darkness of our own shades, shielding our eyes from the bright sunshine, we are not seeing the world in the same way. The following describes our awareness contexts discussed by psychologists Barney Glaser and Anselm Strauss (1965). They describe the different awareness styles, or "awareness contexts," of the dying and the caretaker. Although Glaser and Strauss described situations involving the dying person, I believe that it can be applied to grief situations related to death or other significant losses.

(1) **Closed awareness:**
   All parties are not aware of the facts. In grief situation, they can all be in denial of death itself or they may not be aware of certain information surrounding death.

(2) **Suspected awareness:**
   One party begins to suspect but continues to act as he or she doesn't know.

(3) Mutual-pretense:

All parties know but the information is not shared between them.

(4) Open awareness:

There is a shared openness in communication.

While taking care of someone who was dying, you, the dying, and others may have played different roles in the four awareness contexts. In divorce, perhaps, you and your ex-spouse experienced these different awareness contexts.

A woman loses her father to medical negligence. She and her mother may initially be in *Closed Awareness*, believing that he was given the best medical care. She and her aunt, however, may be in *Suspected Awareness* over what happened. Her aunt suspects negligence and is probing to see if her niece knows. Soon, the niece may also begin to suspect, and she and her aunt will then be in *Mutual Pretense*. One day, they may talk openly and reach *Open Awareness*, yet be still in *Suspect Awareness* with her mother, who they believe is too fragile to face the facts. In some cases, you may never reach *Open Awareness* with all parties. Knowing that the differences exist, however, will help you to be patient with each other's willingness and readiness to face reality.

Glaser, Barney and Strauss, Anselm. (1965). *Awareness of Dying: a Study of Social Interaction.* Chicago, IL: Aldine.

8. Grief Symptoms

Grief is not an illness. Grief is a process of adjusting to the loss of an important relationship, positive or negative. Such a loss can trigger emotions and physical symptoms that may not be characteristic of how you normally react to circumstances. Your friends may become worried and whisper, "Has she (he) gone crazy?" If you had been stoic or emotionally balanced in your life before this loss, the change may be frightening to you and to others. Before you put more pressure on yourself to appear normal, first give yourself the right to have your new feelings.

We may deny that the death or a loss never happened. We may cry our hearts out. We may be angry over small things. We may not be able to think coherently. We may develop infections or suffer from headaches and stomach aches. We may feel that there will be no future happiness. We have strong feelings because (1) we valued and cherished the relationship with the loved one we lost, or (2) we have ambivalence over a person for the way he or she died or lived. These are all normal reactions. The best medicine for grief is the continued love and support coming from family and friends. We all need support when the memory of the funeral or a burial is fading while the sense of loss is still strong within us.

The following reactions can be considered normal grief reactions, provided they are not prolonged or exaggerated:

FEELINGS:
- Sadness, anger, jealousy, fear
- Emotional outbreaks
- Guilt, self-reproach, anxiety
- Loneliness, hopelessness, yearning, numbness, relief

PHYSICAL SYMPTOMS:
- Stomach ache, nausea
- Tightness in the chest or throat
- Shortness of breath
- Appetite disturbances
- Dry mouth
- Menstrual irregularities
- Sleep disturbances
- Oversensitivity to noise
- Fatigue, weak muscles

THOUGHTS:
- Disbelief
- Confusion
- Obsessive thinking
- Lack of focus
- Sense of presence
- Fantasizing

BEHAVIORS:
- Crying, sighing
- Absent-minded behavior
- Dreams of the deceased
- Taking actions so others would not forget the deceased
- Avoiding being reminded of the deceased
- Overplanning (afraid of being alone)
- Treasuring objects that belonged to the deceased
- Carrying objects that remind the survivor of the deceased
- Feeling uneasy about making changes in life
- Being critical of how others grieve
- Social withdrawal

SPIRITUAL REACTIONS (Martin/Doka, 2000)
- ◆ Searching for meaning in loss
- ◆ Changes in spiritual behaviors, feelings, or beliefs

During this period of grief, it helps to have friends who can listen to you without making judgments. It also helps to be able to share your grief with others who are also in pain. The absence of supportive friends and family can make you feel lonely and abandoned. There are, however, other sources of support. Hospitals and hospices offer bereavement sessions where you are invited to talk about your feelings with others.

Although it is normal to have these symptoms during this difficult period, if the symptoms persist over a long time or are exaggerated, please consult a therapist to help you deal with your loss. The next section discusses grief that may require further attention.

Glaser, B., and Strauss, A. (1965). *Awareness of Dying.* Chicago: Adline.

Martin, Terry L. and Doka, Kenneth J. (2000). *Men Don't Cry . . . Women Do.* Philadelphia, PA: Brunner/Mazel.

Rando, Therese A. (1993). *Treatment of Complicated Mourning.* Champaign, IL: Research Press.

Worden, J. William. (1991). *Grief Counseling & Grief Therapy.* New York, NY: Springer Publishing Co.

Keep your face to the sunshine,
and you cannot see
the shadows.

HELEN KELLER

9. Complicated Grief

Complicated grief is grief that is not easily worked out through time and normal support. Its cause may be due to one or more of the following elements:

- ◆ Mourning did not take place.
- ◆ Mourning was delayed, inhibited or distorted.
- ◆ The individual had a conflicted relationship with the deceased. (The relationship with the deceased was troubled or ambivalent.)
- ◆ The loss was unexpected and traumatic, leaning to post-traumatic disorder.
- ◆ There is accumulation of unresolved grief.
- ◆ There is an overload of stress.

Symptoms for complicated grief are similar to the normal reactions to grief listed in Topic 8, but they are usually chronic or more exaggerated in nature. They may also include the following:*

- ◆ Fear of intimacy with others
- ◆ Unusually high death-anxiety about self and others
- ◆ Self-destructive relationship or behavior
- ◆ Chronic anger or depression
- ◆ Radical changes in lifestyle or uncharacteristic show of moods
- ◆ Inability to talk about the deceased
- ◆ Developing physical symptoms similar to those of the deceased
- ◆ Compulsion to imitate the dead person

* Compiled from the works of Worden (1991) and Rando (1993)

WHO ARE AT RISK OF DEVELOPING COMPLICATED GRIEF?

(1) Predisposed factors:
- Young in age
- Poverty
- Low self-esteem
- Difficulty in maintaining relationships
- Past history of multiple losses

(2) Relationship with the deceased:
- Death of a child
- Death of a parent:
  - for a child
  - for an adolescent
  - for an adult
- Death of a sibling
  - for a child
  - for an adolescent
  - for an adult
- Death of a spouse
- Death of a dependent
- Death of a caretaker

(3) Mode of death:
- Unexpected, untimely death
- Very long terminal illness
- Unknown cause or prognosis
- Death seen as preventable
- Bereaved separated in distance physically or emotionally
- Suicide, murder or other violent death

(4) Social support
- ◆ The only child; the only surviving sibling
- ◆ New in the community; no close friends
- ◆ No family nearby, or family seen as inattentive or unapproachable
- ◆ Unsympathetic or insensitive work environment

If many of the above symptoms or risk factors apply to you, there is no need to panic. How we handle grief is unique to the individual, and some can handle an enormous amount of challenges without succumbing to the pressure. It is said that it generally takes two years to feel adjusted to the new way of living. Sigmund Freud calls it a process of cutting off old ties that continues throughout life, while John Bowlby says it is a process of replacing attachments. J. William Worden says that our goal is to reinvent a new future. However we define it, it is not a quick process.

If your grief, however, is preventing you from living a productive life or if your *exaggerated* symptoms are not improving in time, a grief counselor can help you work with the obstacles that are holding you back. Remember that you are the captain of your ship. You also need shipmates to make your journey more comfortable.

Rando, Therese A. (1993). *Treatment of Complicated Mourning.* Champaign, IL: Research Press.

Worden, J. William. (1991). *Grief Counseling & Grief Therapy, a Handbook for the Mental Health Practitioner.* New York, NY: Springer Publishing Company.

Understanding

*I know of no more disagreeable
situation than to be
left feeling generally
angry without
anybody in particular
to be angry at.*

FRANK MOORE COLBY

10. Disenfranchised Grief

There is grief that naturally evokes support. Then there is grief that is muted because of others' fear, disapproval or lack of understanding. This publicly quiet grief is, nevertheless, as painful as those that are accepted by society. The following situations may bring on disenfranchised grief.

- Suicide
- Murder
- Abortion, miscarriage, and stillborns
- Divorce or a break-up in a relationship
- AIDS
- Sudden Infant Death Syndrome
- Missing children
- Extramarital affair (death of a lover)
- Dysfunctional family relationships
- Pet Loss

If you lost your father who was well-respected in the community, you will find strong support coming your way. What if he had been homeless and an alcoholic? Or if he had died in jail from having committed an unspeakable crime? Will you have the same amount of social support? Probably not.

If you lose your lover whose relationship with you is not recognized by law or by society, you will probably not mourn publicly or openly. Your culture or religion may not recommend a ceremony for a death of a newborn, and the grief may become a silent and haunting remembrance in you. A pet loss is often not understood by those who don't own pets. Pets are family members, sometimes more devoted and sensitive than people are, and their loss can be great.

Divorce produces grief. Opportunities for a healthy closure are often denied since one spouse can close the door to the past before any understanding is reached. To grieve for a death of a relationship that simultaneously demands a new relationship is often a very difficult task. Often, for the sake of children's happiness, many of us pretend to lead a pain-free life in the post-divorce world.

For all of our losses, sanctioned or not sanctioned by society, we must handle our grief personally and individually. Regardless of how the individual lived at the time of his or her death, there is now a void.

You may be facing the death of someone who had hurt you a lot in your life. Death ends the physical connection, but the bond is still there. If the relationship was painful and dysfunctional, you may have a complex set of emotions coming from relief, regrets, anger and other feelings. In such cases, you must find a symbolic way of letting go. Express your feelings openly or privately on paper if there is no one to listen to you.

No matter how society may interpret your relationship with the deceased, your emotions are real. The unresolved feelings you harbor will only hurt you, not the deceased. The guilt you may feel for not being sad will only bother you, not the deceased. While the person was living, there was at least an object for your anger. It's as if you were practicing tennis against a wall, and suddenly the wall was removed. Where do you throw the ball now? At your next door neighbor's window? Light a candle and talk to the "unreachable." If possible, keep a memory box of items that remind you of the good times you've shared.

11. Children and Grief

We are not certain when grief became identified as an adult behavior, but research indicates that children do grieve although in a somewhat different way. It is important to understand the way psychologists view children's grief since how we treat children who are in grief can affect their adult life. They, too, feel the loss. They, too, have the need to express feelings and share mourning.

Freud, Erikson and Piaget have defined human development in stages, as identified below. Can we also assume that children's grief patterns follow such schemes?

Sigmund Freud (1905)	Erik Erikson (1963)	Jean Piaget (1952, 1962)
Oral	Trust vs. Mistrust	Sensorimotor
Anal	Initiative vs. Guilt	Preoperational
Phallic	Industry vs. Inferiority	Concrete Operational
Latency	Identity vs. Confusion	Formal Operational
Genital	Intimacy vs. Isolation	
(adolescence to	Generativity vs. Stagnation	
adult)	Ego-integrity vs. Despair	

THINGS TO CONSIDER:

(1) Two interesting research results:

Maria Nagy (1948/59): Studied 378 children aged 3 - 10 in Budapest, Hungary, in the 1930s.

Less than 5: Death is reversible, not final. Death is just "less alive."

5 - 9: Death is personified and final. (Less personification shown in recent years.) You can hide from death.

| 9 - 10: | Death is final, inevitable, personal, and universal. |

Gerald Koocher (1973) applied Piaget's developmental stages and confirmed Nagy's research results. He, however, believed that maturation level was more significant than age. According to Robert Kastenbaum (2000), most researchers still agree with the basic findings of Maria Nagy.

Kastenbaum (1998) describes the reaction of a 16-month to the death of a caterpillar. The boy calls out "No more" and later shows sadness and distress. Life was somehow "no more." Other cases show that young children can sense and experience the loss associated with death.

Myra Bluebond-Langner (1977): Studied hospitalized, terminally-ill children on death awareness.

Bluebond-Langner found that dying children, as young as 18-month-olds, can be aware of their impending death, seen through personal experiences and through the reactions of those who surround them.

(2) Questions children may be asking:

"Is it my fault?" or "Did I cause it?"
"Is it going to happen to me?"
"Who will to take care of me now?"

(3) How children's grief may be similar or different:

Children may differ in how they grieve, but what they need is not different from what we adults need:

- ◆ Listen to what they are saying and look for cues.
- ◆ Give them freedom to express their thoughts and emotions.
- ◆ Commemorate the loss with them.

Children may need special considerations:

- ◆ Their attention span is short.
- ◆ They may quickly switch from one emotion to another.
- ◆ They will revisit their grief at different developmental stages throughout life. In other words, their grief *ripens* with age.
- ◆ They should be given a choice on whether or not to attend the funeral.
- ◆ They need reassurance that there will always be someone to take care of them.
- ◆ Art and music are good tools of expression.

(4) Children's grief signs:

- ◆ Separation anxiety
- ◆ Fear of abandonment
- ◆ Overdependency
- ◆ Guilt
- ◆ Crying, depression
- ◆ Lower grades
- ◆ Lower attendance rate
- ◆ Over-achievement
- ◆ Somatic complaints (physical pain)
- ◆ Sleep disorders
- ◆ Eating disorders
- ◆ Aggressive behavior
- ◆ Social withdrawal

Engler, Barbara. (1999). *Personality Theories.* New York, NY: Houghton Mifflin.

Feldman, Robert S. (2000). *Development Across the Lifespan.* New Jersey: Prentice-Hall.

Kastenbaum, Robert. (1998). *Death, Society, and Human Experience.* Needham Heights, MA: Allyn and Bacon.

Kastenbaum, Robert. (2000). *The Psychology of Death.* New York, NY: Springer Publishing.

Koocher, Gerald. (1973). *Developmental Psychology*, 9, 369-375. Childhood, Death, and Cognitive Development

Worden, J. William (1991). *Grief Counseling & Grief Therapy.* New York, NY: Springer Publishing.

*A bit of fragrance always
clings to the hand
that gives roses.*

CHINESE PROVERB

12. The Elderly and Grief

We have learned that children's grief is revisited and reviewed at different periods during their life span. By the time these same children become elderly, their grief experience is rich.

Let's assume that we begin collecting rocks as a child. Periodically, we look inside the bag and find something that interests us in the collection. By the time we're 80, we have quite a collection of rocks: smooth or jagged; colorful or dull; pleasing or repulsive. Some of us who studied geology know that rocks are sedimentary, igneous or metamorphic, depending on how they were formed. Some have layers, and some have speckles. Some crumble. Some are as hard as diamonds. Similarly, our appreciation for death experience depends on where we've walked; what we've collected along the path; and the pressure, heat and erosion that molded, shaped and added texture to our death experiences — our rocks.

UNIQUENESS OF THE ELDERLY'S GRIEF:

- ◆ *Diminishing support:*

  We expand our circle of friends and family throughout life, but at sometime, if we live long enough, we begin to see a reverse effect taking place. Our circle of support begins to shrink in size.

- ◆ *Grief overload — an overwhelming accumulation of death experiences:*

  The elderly can experience death of their children, spouses, relatives and friends within a short length of time. There is not enough time to work through each loss.

- ◆ *Personal vulnerability in the newly found role:*

  Life is changed suddenly when the caretaker dies, or the person he or she is caring for dies. Death of a spouse can mean instant loneliness.

- ◆ *Personal death awareness:*
  Deaths of others in the same age group, same social group or in similar situations make their own death more real and imminent.

- ◆ *Relocation:*
  Death of a spouse may necessitate relocation, which requires adjustment and can cause additional stress.

- ◆ *Loss of meaning in life:*
  Retirement can remove the need to plan their future. The physical process of aging can also result in more sickness. They may feel that their future is grim. The elderly can experience depression.

WHAT WE CAN DO TO HELP THE ELDERLY IN GRIEF:

- ◆ They may have a need to be touched, especially after losing a spouse. Look for cues and provide them with a touch, e.g., a hug, a kiss on the cheek, a pat on the shoulder, a hand shake.
- ◆ They may have a need to reminisce. Take time out to sit with them and go through their albums. It will be mutually enjoyable.
- ◆ Encourage them to revisit old interests and start new ones. Introduce new topics into their lives.
- ◆ Look for signs of depression. They may need medication, exercise or therapy.

If we consider Erikson's developmental scheme (see topic 11), the last stage in life is "Ego Integrity vs. Despair." How we deal with life and grief at this stage in life is affected by how we have learned to deal with our past experiences. We cannot rearrange others' past for them, but we can certainly be good listeners and appreciate where they are in life.

13. Pet Loss

Compared to human age span, the majority of our pets can't outlive us. Thus, in our life time, we will say good-bye to the little creatures who give us joy and comfort.

HOW CAN WE NOT GRIEVE FOR THE LOSS OF . . .

- Our dog greeting us at the door, a habit we took for granted

- Our dog whose big eyes asked, "What's wrong?" and treated us with her wet kisses

- Our cat that brushed against me as I cooked at the stove

- Our dog stealing food from the bin without realizing that his tummy could not hold more food

- Our ferret who loved to steal beer and party with us

- Our cat purring one moment and hissing the next, always doing her own thing

- Our parakeet who dirtied the cage but never learned a word

- Our ferret with the musky scent, who routinely stole shiny objects and hid them under the bed

- Our grandmother's dog who guarded her body after she fell down from a stroke

- Our Siberian hamster who would always peek her head out of her bed the moment her name was called, who also survived being caught by the mouse trap, or who pretended to be dead when the cat knocked down the cage

- Our friend's crow whose death revealed a box full of shiny, expensive jewelry he had stolen from neighbors' houses

- Our classroom pet guinea pig, Charlie Brown, who once shared his bed with the school field mouse

145

Pet losses can be as difficult as human losses because they are our trusted companions. They often give unconditional love and an unbeatable sense of loyalty that we sometimes don't find in humans. Thus, when a pet is lost or dies, our grief can be great. We grieve for the loss of a very important family member. We have the right to express our feelings that come only from the fact that we simply loved them, and they loved us.

There is no psychiatrist in the world like a puppy licking your face.

BEN WILLIAMS

Rainbow Bridge

Just this side of heaven is a place called Rainbow Bridge.

When an animal dies that has been especially close to someone here, that pet goes to Rainbow Bridge. There are meadows and hills for all of our special friends so they can run and play together. There is plenty of food, water and sunshine, and our friends are warm and comfortable.

All the animals who had been ill and old are restored to health and vigor. Those who were hurt or maimed are made whole and strong again, just as we remember them in our dreams of days and times gone by. The animals are happy and content, except for one small thing: they each miss someone very special to them, who had to be left behind.

They all run and play together, but the day comes when one suddenly stops and looks into the distance. His bright eyes are intent. His eager body quivers. Suddenly he begins to run from the group, flying over the green grass, his legs carrying him faster and faster.

You have been spotted, and when you and your special friend finally meet, you cling together in joyous reunion, never to be parted again. The happy kisses rain upon your face; your hands again caress the beloved head, and you look once more into the trusting eyes of your pet, so long gone from your life but never absent from your heart.

Then you cross Rainbow Bridge together . . .

Author unknown . . .

I am fond of pigs.
Dogs look up to us.
Cats look down.
Pigs treat us as equals.

WINSTON CHURCHILL

14. Multicultural Interest

Grief is internal and personal, whereas mourning is external and often cultural. The world seems to be getting smaller with the instant communication afforded by computers. Yet when it comes to our understanding of grief, the differences still remain separated by the cultural groups to which we belong. Perhaps the only way to break that barrier is to study and appreciate the differences that surround what is really a very common and shared aspect of life — grief over the loss of someone we loved.

A century ago, it was much easier to know our expectations of mourning. We accepted the religious beliefs of our parents and ancestors. Our concept of life and death were handed to us early in our life. Living in fairly isolated communities, we knew our traditions and the social rules of mourning. Living in the 21st century, however, we are exposed to many cultures from which our families and friends come. That makes our mourning difficult. We need to look at the cultural differences without mocking them. All cultures, including our own, have some strange elements to them when we look at them from the outside. Here are some *"Did you know that?"* which might interest you. They are only glimpses of the diversity in traditions.

DID YOU KNOW THAT . . .

. . . The fear of being buried alive in some cultures led to stimulating the deceased's body (poking, washing, wailing, or even decapitating)?

DID YOU KNOW THAT . . .

. . . There is evidence that the Neanderthals stained their dead with red ocher, which could indicate their belief in life-after-death?

DID YOU KNOW THAT . . .

. . . There is much diversity within the Christian community on funeral and burial traditions or their beliefs on what happens after one dies?

. . . There is variance in the acceptance of cremation, the use of music during a funeral, and even in their belief in the concept of heaven and hell?

DID YOU KNOW THAT . . .

. . . Our world and diverse cultures have buried our beloved in the following ways: cremation, earth burial, exposure, water burial, and cannibalism?

DID YOU KNOW THAT . . .

. . . In some cultures, mourners unrelated to the deceased are hired to wail and grieve?

. . . How we grieve at a funeral may not indicate how we grieve personally away from the funeral?

DID YOU KNOW THAT . . .

. . . Quakers hold memorial services several weeks after death in order to honor the deceased?

. . . A folder with a picture of the deceased and a description is organized for the service?

DID YOU KNOW THAT . . .

. . . Many Native American tribes see the butterfly as a symbol of everlasting life?

DID YOU KNOW THAT . . .

. . . In Mormon belief, life goes forward and backward, and that learning continues to take place after death?

DID YOU KNOW THAT . . .

. . . The African Americans in New Orleans have what is called a "Jazz Funeral," where there is first a funeral (a rite of passage), a procession toward the cemetery called "dirge," then a "cutting the body loose" (a farewell to the deceased at the cemetery), and a "joyous send off" or "second line" once the body is buried?

. . . The dirge is a calm, slow movement, and the second line is a joyous marching, all done with the band and the passers-by joining in?

DID YOU KNOW THAT . . .

. . . Japanese send money called "okōden" to the family of the deceased to help defray the funeral cost, and that the family reciprocates by sending small gifts?

Understanding

DID YOU KNOW THAT . . .

> . . . The Lakota tribe mourns with an unrestrained expression of grief by both men and women, and that gifts of money and food are offered?
>
> . . . The family feeds the mourners and humorous stories are told?
>
> . . . The deceased's possessions are either given away or burned?

DID YOU KNOW THAT . . .

> . . . Those of Islamic faith have professional washers, and the deceased is washed three times?
>
> . . . God sends an "angel of death" to help remove the soul from the body at the time of death?
>
> . . . Complete silence is encouraged during funerals?

DID YOU KNOW THAT . . .

> . . . Crying is not encouraged during Buddhist funerals?
>
> . . . Death is not sorrowful since without death there would be no reincarnation?
>
> . . . The 49th day after death is very important to Buddhists?

DID YOU KNOW THAT . . .

> . . . In Hinduism, "karma" is a basic law of the mind, a "cause and effect" of life?
>
> . . . The rebirth is governed by "karma"?
>
> . . . There are different levels of "heaven"?
>
> . . . The family can sit around during the cremation period?

DID YOU KNOW THAT . . .

> . . . Hmongs have funeral rituals traditionally lasting three full days; announce death by the sound of a rifle; sacrifice animals; and prepare and serve meals for the dead and the living?
>
> . . . A bamboo reed (mouth organ) called "Qeej" has a special role in sending the soul back to the ancestors, preparing it for the next life, and to help those who are still living?

DID YOU KNOW THAT . . .

> . . . The Jews bury the deceased within 24 hours, except on the Sabbath, in a simple wooden box?
>
> . . . The first week of mourning is called Shiva, and that friends and relatives bring food and comfort to the bereaved?
>
> . . . The Rabbi or a representative tears the blouse or shirt of the mourners as a symbol of their torn or broken heart?

DID YOU KNOW THAT . . .

> . . . The active and retired members of the United States Navy and their dependents are entitled to burial at sea?

DID YOU KNOW THAT . . .

> . . . Funeral parlors in England can be found on city streets, and some have offices in the hospitals?

DID YOU KNOW THAT . . .

> . . . The crematorium can be found next to the chapel, disguised, in English funeral parlors?

Understanding

DID YOU KNOW THAT . . .

> . . . Romani (or "gypsies") have their own funeral traditions, where their grief may be expressed by moaning, shouting, throwing themselves on the floor or even scratching their faces?

DID YOU KNOW THAT . . .

> . . . The earlier Buddhist priests in Japan did not perform funerals, while funerals and Buddhist priests are synonymous in modern Japan?

DID YOU KNOW THAT . . .

> . . . Some cultures have gender biases on burials?
> . . . According to "History of Funeral Customs," published by the Wyoming Funeral Directors Association, men and women were treated differently at death; e.g., Cochieans burying their women but suspending their men from trees, Ghonods burying their women but cremating their men, or Bongas burying their men facing north and their women facing south?

Recommended Reading:

Parry, Joan K. and Ryan, Angela Shen. (1995). *A Cross-cultural Look at Death, Dying, and Religion.* Chicago, IL: Nelson-Hall Publishers.

Internet References:

Deal, S. (1998). Contemporary English Cemeteries. [Online internet], available: http://home.flash.net/~leimer/england.html

Falk, C. (1992). Hmong Funeral in Australia in 1992. [Online Internet], available: http://www.hmongnet.org/hmong-au/funeral.htm

Funeral Rites and Customs (2001). [Online Internet, Encarta Learning Zone], available: http://www.encarta.msn.com/find/Concise.asp?z= 1&pg=2&ti=761565630

Umehara, Takeshi (Vol. 16, #3, Autumn, 1989). The Japanese view of the hereafter. [Online Internet], available: http://www.japanecho.co.jp

Ryczak, K., Zebreski, L., May, M., Traver, S., & Kemp, C. (October 12, 2000). Gypsy (Roma): Health Care, Beliefs and Practices. [Online Internet], available: http://www.baylor.edu/~Charles_Kemp/ gypsy_health.htm

Sacred Text Archive. (2001). [Online Internet], available: http://www.sacred-texts.com/index.htm

Wyoming Funeral Directors Association—History of Funeral Customs (2000) [Online Internet], available: http://www.wyfda.org

Yale University Library Research Guide - Hinduism. (2001) [Online Internet], available: http://www.library.yale.edu/rsc/religion/hindu.htm

*A smile is a curve that
sets everything straight.*

PHYLLIS DILLER

COMFORTING WORDS

How others have learned to cope with their losses

Sue Adams

Roberta Rook

Linda Scott

Lauren MacBlane

Deborah Boggs

Cathy Campbell

Kei Gilbert

Ray Scheck

Trisha Kiyohara

*People are like
stained-glass windows.
They sparkle and shine
when the sun is out,
but when the darkness sets in,
their beauty is revealed
only if there is
a light from within.*

ELISABETH KÜBLER-ROSS

Sue Adams
College Program Administrator

MARY'S LEGACY

The call came at 11:38 PM. My husband, Mike, and I had just gotten to sleep after a busy workday when the bedside phone rang.

"Hello, may I speak with Mike Adams, please?" came the male voice in a matter-of-fact tone. I handed the phone to my groggy spouse and wondered who would call at such an hour.

"Hello?" croaked Mike, then dropped his eyes as he heard the caller's message. After a long moment, he choked, "What about Mom?"

There had been an accident. Mike's dad had fallen asleep at the wheel of his van, and as his foot sunk further on the gas pedal, they had driven off the road, hitting a telephone pole. Mike's mother had not survived the impact.

As he handed back the phone to be replaced in the receiver, I saw my rock of a husband collapse. I had never seen him collapse before.

Earlier that June day, Mike had picked up his parents, Frank and Mary Adams, from the Portland Airport as they returned from a month-long "dream trip" to Europe. After years of saving and struggling to raise seven children, it had been his mother's lifelong desire to visit her family's Irish homeland and to see the cathedrals and historical sights of Europe. Mike's dad, however, had been less enthusiastic about the prospect of such a trip, saying he'd seen "too much of the world" during the war years. But, always the supportive husband, Frank was pleased to give Mary her dream.

When they arrived at our home from the airport, we ordered Chinese take-out and spent a leisurely couple of hours listening to Mary excitedly telling of their adventures in Europe, her blue eyes sparkling as she spoke between bites of chow mein and fried shrimp. By eight o'clock, Frank and Mary prepared to leave for the 90-minute drive south to their Corvallis home. We invited them to stay; since there was a sofa-sleeper in the family room, why drive home after such a long plane trip? They thought not. They had driven home from Portland so many times before, after family visits and opera performances; to them, it seemed just a short jaunt. And they were ready, after such a long journey, to sleep in their own bed.

So they transferred their luggage from our car to their van, which had been parked at our house while they were away. We hugged good-bye and planned to get together on the weekend to see the photographs Mary had taken on the trip. She was on cloud nine, full of delight at what she had experienced. Mike and I were delighted to see her so happy.

Then came the phone call. Was it real? Couldn't be. We returned a call to the hospital emergency room just to be sure we'd heard correctly.

My God, it was true.

Stunned, Mike was somehow able to drive the 45 miles to the small-town hospital where his father had been taken. At his father's request, Mike stoically pulled his parents' belongings from the crushed van and handled business with the hospital. When he arrived home in the wee hours of the morning, there were phone calls to be made to his six siblings. And when the sun finally rose, we set our school-aged daughters on the foot of our unkept bed and told them their grandmother had died.

Within a day, Mike's sisters and brothers arrived in Portland from points across the country looking exhausted and pale. Local friends donated boxes of Kleenex and volunteered to make airport runs and bring food. Corvallis friends spread the news and prepared the way for the family to arrive back in town.

Frank, miraculously uninjured, was discharged from the hospital to our home, where he and his children spent the next morning both weeping and roaring with laughter as they recalled Mom in the process of writing her obituary. Two days after the accident, this abundant family saddled up for the trip to Corvallis and in a caravan of rented and borrowed cars, took their father home.

I'll never forget the raucous round-table meeting facilitated by the family priest where 17 of us sat in a big circle on the back patio of the family home and shared our memories of Mom. We heard how Mary took food to the poor and the ill, her nursing career, how she lingered too long in museums, and liked things done "just so" in the kitchen. We recalled her dedication to her family, church and community, as well as her infectious laugh, and Sunday dinners of Mom's roast-"beast." My young daughters later commented that they'd learned more about their grandmother that day than they'd known about her when she was alive.

The days that followed seemed an endless parade of flowers, friends, and food. Those who had felt her care in difficult times were there to remember her and to support her family in our difficult times. It was a powerful paradox of love and sadness, of comfort and pain, of laughter and tears.

Although those who loved her were overwhelmed by this sudden and devastating loss, they agreed that it could not be considered a tragedy. Even as her family grieved, they knew that when a life is lived well, thoroughly lived with teeth sunk in, heart and mind engaged, then it is not a tragedy when that life is over. And Mary had really lived her life, savored it, worked at it, delighted in it, and she left the world better as a result. In the months before she died, she had seen a daughter married and enjoyed the family reunion that followed; she had gazed with awe at the Sistine Chapel, castles on the Rhine, the ruins of Pompeii, and St. Peter's Basilica. We had expected her to live to at least 90 — age 72 seemed much too young — but hers was a well-lived life nonetheless, and her death could not be considered a tragedy.

In the days that followed the accident, Mike didn't have time to cry, and he's never been the type to talk much about his feelings. Instead, he spent hour upon hour lovingly carving a wooden cross to place at the scene of the accident. And the day before his siblings departed for their respective homes in New York, Texas and California, they made a pilgrimage to the site. It had happened just outside the tiny town of Amity, Oregon, in a Hazelnut orchard surrounded by fields. There were no building to be seen, only well-tended trees and across the way, rolling hills, majestic mountains beyond. As Mike placed the cross and his sisters propped a bountiful bouquet of flowers, a truck driver honked and a few passers-by waved. Even strangers cared.

Mary was my husband's mother, not mine, and though I cared for her deeply, I cannot claim to understand what it is like to lose a parent. My grief has also been real, though it is different from that of my husband, and a great portion of my grief has been in watching him suffer. Mary was my mother-in-law, but she was also a friend. Often at family gatherings, she and I would linger at the breakfast table, sipping cold coffee while debating the problems of the world and the meaning of life. The rest of the family would have rolled their eyes and left the table long since, but she and I would just stay and talk and talk. I miss her.

It's now been four years since Mary died. At times, my husband still tears up when he thinks of her, and we occasionally experience a pang of guilt wondering if things might have turned out differently had we urged them to stay at our home rather than drive home that night. And I must admit that writing this has been difficult, though the memories it has aroused have been strangely more good than bad. Four new Adams grandchildren have been born since she died, and though they will know their grandmother only from the stories and photographs their parents, aunts and uncles share when they get together, they carry a part of her within them. Life goes on.

Mike and I have moved from Oregon to Maryland, and our kids are now teenagers. Funny, but we still startle at the sound of a late night phone call. And now that our eldest daughter is driving, we worry that she is safe. Life is tenuous, after all. But to let fear rule our lives wouldn't be the message that Mary would want us to take from this. Rather, we remind ourselves that though we cannot know what the future holds, we can choose to savor each day as Mary did, to say the things that need to be said, to go to the places we dream of going, and to show our families and friends that we love them every day. That is Mary's legacy.

Roberta Rook
Psychotherapist

GRIEF: A PERSONAL ODYSSEY

Although this comparison is by no means intended to sound pretentious, there are two distinct periods of my life that parallel those of the pre-Christian (B.C.) and post-Christian (A.D.) world. These periods comprise my life before the deaths of my parents, and my life afterwards. For as the world was changed forever upon the arrival and subsequent death of Christ, so was my world changed forever by the personally cataclysmic events of the summer of '96. And, as Christ's death was redemptive for scores of humanity, so these deaths, particularly that of my mother, were redemptive for me. I died to the world I knew, only to be reborn — transformed, metamorphosed.

My father died after a long period of chronic illness and a relatively short period of terminal illness. My relationship with him was complex, difficult, at many times tortuous. My mother died 34 days after my father, despite the fact they'd been separated for 30 years. Her death was accidental, shocking — an elderly man in a pick-up truck hit her as she walked the country road in front of her house one foggy Virginia morning. My relationship with her was close, sometimes overpowering for one who'd learned that there was safety from the intensity of both parents in emotional restraint.

With my father's passing, I began to have personal acquaintance with death. With my mother's death, I was plunged headlong into the surreal world of traumatic loss. I'd gone from a primer in death to the equivalent of advanced doctoral training in little over a month. I now had the dubious distinction of being in the club of *"Those Who Got the Phone Call."*

The grief experts tell us that we move through our initial disbelief regarding our loss — this is the initial task to be mastered in grief. However, let me state **adamantly** that I have not, in nearly four years, been able to completely shake the nightmarish quality of first hearing of my mother's accident. It is a feeling that I do not think will ever completely leave me. The true ramifications of my mother's dying the way she died still retain their power to shock me when I allow them into my consciousness. At times it is as if my **coping** with her loss has been the Great Lie, the ultimate denial, and that this state, rather than my old grief state, has been the dream from which I must eventually awaken.

This, of course, is part of the paradox of grief. Grief is instinctive and adaptive, and we as mere mortals must survive loss; yet to exist in this world, we must largely deny the personal reality of death. (It won't happen now, not to ourselves or the ones we love.) We turn to others in the face of loss, yet grief more than anything makes us face our complete isolation as unique individuals, our existential aloneness. We try to reconcile two worlds — the world we once knew and the world that will be as we make a new life for ourselves. We know the world that was and at times may find comfort there, but the world of our future is difficult to construct, and in its final outcome, out of our hands. Personally, grief has taught me that I can only reconcile these worlds imperfectly but that I can live fully in the present, realizing that life is to be savored, time is of the essence, and that, ultimately, love is all we take from this world and the only legacy we can leave it.

How far that little candle
throws his beams!
So shines a good deed
in a weary world.

SHAKESPEARE

Linda Scott, Ph.D.
Professor of Psychology
Hood College

A DRESS REHEARSAL

I was 26 years old, and my mother was dying of lung cancer, although this was 25 years ago and none of us in the family used that word openly to each other or to my mother. I was working in Maryland and flew to Florida as soon as the academic semester ended to help my father and brother care for my mother. The night that I arrived, my father asked me to sleep in the room with my mother because he had a bad cold, and he didn't want to give it to her. I was very tired, and as soon as I rested my head on the pillow, I began to fall asleep, only to drift into a dream. Since my mother was in a lot of pain and needed pain medication every four hours, I slept lightly next to her.

The next morning, my mother was in a lot of pain and was having trouble breathing. She asked us to call her doctor, and the doctor directed us to have her taken to the hospital by ambulance. We had a long and difficult wait in the ER as the doctors tried to stabilize her and to give her pain relief. After a while, a doctor came out to tell us that she had died. It was a painful and unreal time for us.

Later, I was still feeling the shock of what seemed to be such a painful and ugly death for my beautiful mother. Suddenly, I remembered the dream I had the night before my mother's death. In the dream, I was one of a group of people helping brides to dress for their weddings. There was much hustling, but with a sense of peace and joy. We were arranging the long flowing dress and train for the bride, with the sense that the woman we were preparing was to be the next to be married. Then the dream ended.

As I thought over this dream, I felt a sense of wonder and peace, which has returned to me every time I remember this dream. In my grief, it seemed she was taken from us so painfully and unnaturally, but the dream gave me an image of a natural and joyous transition for my mother. I am profoundly grateful that this dream came to me.

> *Do what you can,*
> *with what you have,*
> *where you are.*
>
> THEODORE ROOSEVELT

Lauren MacBlane
Jewelry Designer

GIDGET - "THE BESTEST PUPPY EVER"

"Gidget, the Bestest Puppy Ever" is what my husband and I told her more than once a day because she was that. She was my Christmas present from David because I wanted a companion, a lively presence for a house in which I spent a lot of time alone. How wrong I was to think we were just getting a dog to come home to. She quickly became a child for a childless couple. We made excuses to our friends so we could hang out with Gidget. We stopped going out to eat to avoid leaving her alone at home. If we did go somewhere, we couldn't wait to see her no matter how long we were gone — five minutes or five hours. She was with us for only four brief months, yet I will always be amazed at the magnitude of her impact on us.

When the vet called to tell us Gidget did not survive her spaying operation, I truly thought he called the wrong person. He could not be talking about our Gidget. She was fine, wondering where we disappeared to because she wanted to go home! I called my husband at work and said, "Gidget is not alive any more," because I couldn't say she was dead. How do you tell someone that? We went to the vet to see her and say goodbye. She looked asleep, not dead, and she felt warm and alive. See, I thought, I knew he made a mistake.

I couldn't believe this was happening. It was very surreal because it was so unexpected. I had pretended all day not to be worried. I was doing the right thing. She was supposed to be home the next day looking at me through the window while I was pulling weeds. She was supposed to be sitting by the refrigerator to get her ice cube treat when David mixed his evening cocktail. She was supposed to be snoozing on the end of the couch while we watched a movie.

The night she died, we put all her things in a box because we could not look at them. We wrote down everything we loved about her and all her special ways because we never wanted to forget her. We had to stop because the tears got thick and we were feeling worse.

These tears were our constant companions for the next few days. David and I took turns — he would cry and I would soothe him, and then I would wail and he would comfort me. More than once, we cried together when we both were overwhelmed with sadness. We talked to her and about her endlessly for three or four days. David did not go to work. What would have been the point? I knew the intensity of our sadness would lessen as time passed. Though I hate to wish time away, I really wanted it to go by so I could inch toward feeling better. Looking back, I still can't believe how awful we both felt. Of course, time did not hurry for us; rather, it moved forward in slow motion. After about three or four long days, however, the extreme sadness began to recede and the weight of our numbness began to lighten.

As we began feeling better, which was really just feeling less bad, we knew we needed to mark her life with us in a special way. We learned, on the Internet, of a ceremony held every Monday night at 10:00 where people around the world light a candle for their pets that have died. We decided that we would use this night to say our goodbyes to Gidget. We set out her favorite toys and some treats and lit our candle. We both told her how much we loved her and missed her. We told her how special she will always be to us, and we remembered out loud some of our fondest memories of her time with us. We cried a lot more tears and when the candle was flickering out, we said our final goodbye. The ceremony was emotionally upsetting yet extremely helpful to our healing process. For us, this ritual made losing Gidget feel more real and less dreamlike. It also created a singular memory of our farewell to our first puppy whose memories were her best gift to us.

Before we had her cremated, we also had the vet snip hair from her beautiful curlicue tail, from her eye area to get her tear stains and from her ears because they were such a wonderful shade of apricot. Gidget's ashes sit on David's dresser on top of a keepsake box with her favorite purple bug, a liver treat (her yummiest), her hair and her collar. She has a larger special box with all her other toys, her blanket, her chewed up brush with her hair ensnarled in the teeth, and her bowl engraved in humor by her friends with "Gidget — Daddy's Little Girl."

During the first week of our grief, David wrote a song he could sing to her every night so she would know we didn't forget her. David swore he would sing her song to her every night, tell her how much we loved and missed her, and how much she meant to us. He did this faithfully for a few weeks, and each night, we cried more tears. Four months later, David rarely sings her song or talks to her aloud and feels okay. We are comfortable with our sometimes occasional and sometimes frequent thoughts of her. We are grateful that when we think or speak of her, we mostly smile and only occasionally cry.

While we grieved, we talked a lot about being able to prepare for a loved one's death versus being shocked with tragedy. I lost my father to a long illness and when he died, I felt like I had been grieving for years, so death seemed less awful. I still felt terrible and cheated but was glad he was not suffering any more. He was somewhere better than the hell he was living alive. Losing Gidget so suddenly rocked me in a way I never could have prepared for. How and why would I? Death seems much more dreadful and sad when it comes suddenly and unexpectedly. I have always wished to be hit by a truck for a quick death, but I selfishly don't want anyone I love to die that way — I want to say "Good bye."

Another aspect of managing our grief was our desire to get another dog. We had the opportunity to get a cousin of hers who would be ready to be brought home two weeks after we lost "The Gidge." We asked everyone we knew, dog people and not-dog-people, for their insight. Do we wait or plunge into puppy love again? We heard as many opinions as people we asked. We had so many concerns — would we forget Gidget, would we expect the new puppy to be just like her, would we expect her to be completely different, would we be able to love her enough, etc. After considerable thought, we decided to get another puppy — her cousin whom we named Georgia Gem. We also threw our normal caution out the door and brought home Mister Buddy, Georgia's brother.

Sometimes, our new puppies make us cry about Gidget but mostly, they remind us of how much we loved her and what a great dog she was. We adore our new puppies as much as Gidget and comparing their antics to Gidget's actually makes us happy, not sad. They are each a little bit like her but mostly they are just themselves. We laugh instead of cry when they do something Gidget would have done, and we laugh when they do something completely new. We are sure that we will always have dogs and that each new dog will remind us of those that were our pets before them.

Our grief for Gidget still touches us as powerfully as her brief presence in our lives affected us. Rarely are there days we don't think of her and our love for her. She made us realize how much love we could give and how changing our life could be so easy. In life, she was a companion, a friend and a teacher. In death, she remains a teacher for she taught us to be happy with our memories of her life and to be content with our sadness over her death.

Love, like death, changed everything.

KAHLIL GIBRAN

Deborah Boggs
Nurse Practitioner

AS DEATH BECOMES MORE PERSONAL

Open caskets, closed caskets, wakes, plain plywood coffins, cremations, funeral homes, churches, gravesite ceremonies, caskets lowering into the ground, memorial services weeks later, funerals within 48 hours, flat markers, tombstones, wills, living wills, donations of one's body to the living and to science . . .

I find that in my 50s, I have now had some personal experience of each of these traditions and ways of noting the death of another. Some were intimate experiences with family, some with friends, others less intimate with acquaintances or coworkers. All, however, have a cumulative effect in shaping one's feelings and beliefs about death. Some deaths, such as my elderly grandmother with Alzheimer's, seem like a relief. She had long stopped talking or recognizing anyone and remained a living shell of one who had already left us years earlier. We had done much of our grieving and preparation before her death. Other deaths have felt untimely as friends of mine grieved for the children who never had the chance to live their lives, dying at birth. Some deaths, such as my grandparents, evolved slowly with declining health. The death became inevitable and we could prepare ourselves. My father was killed suddenly and violently when he was struck by a speeding motorist at age 61. That death shocked my soul and took me months and months to delve through the layers of grief.

Before this year, however, death somehow stayed outside of me. Death came appropriately to the older generation — grandparents, uncles, great aunts. Orderly, in its place. Or death struck the young and innocent, or adult acquaintances. Or it was a random auto accident. This year, though, death found two close friends. Not acquaintances, but close friends. My generation, my contemporaries. ME? And not a random car accident, but an illness. Cancer, and a heart attack. Older people's diseases. How closely death has approached me.

So, I come to the year's end, feeling the loss of both Barry and Bernice. I have a new level of awareness of the brevity and preciousness of life, a renewed sense of intention of how to spend what time I have left. I also find myself wondering about what is helpful and not helpful in preparing for and then dealing with one's own death and the death of others. I learned from the unexpected and sudden deaths of my father and stepmother and friends that I must not postpone decisions and documents. My husband and I prepared wills and powers of attorney, etc., last year, hopefully to save our children from dealing with a legal mess and with uncertainty at a time when they should only deal with their grief. I have learned how important it is to talk about what exists and where it exists and to talk about what one wants in relation to one's own death. My friend died a peaceful death at home and spared unnecessary and pointless medical intervention this year because her son and daughter, only in their twenties, knew what their mother wanted. I learned from all this.

I wonder about our varied religious and cultural traditions and our personal choices in celebrating and mourning the passing of a loved one. I was raised going to memorial services — no casket, no body. It looked like any other day in church, far different from the open casket wake of my Roman Catholic co-worker's husband. Far different, too, from the gravesite ceremony of my Jewish friends, throwing dirt on the casket. The Quaker services that I now claim as my spiritual home are enriching in the spontaneous sharing of stories and memories of the one who has died. I can see value, though, in the tangible evidence of death in the grave, the casket. Death can often feel unreal without the concrete evidence before us. Yet, the rush to arrange the funeral can overwhelm a family with details when perhaps all they really should do is just sit and weep and share memories.

In a community, however, we can hold up one another in our grief, in the arranging of the details of funerals and of finances and of life. We can support one another through an illness, long or short. We can be there for the widow or the motherless child. However we celebrate and memorialize a death, we need to do it with each other. We need to be open and honest with one another in life so that we can part freely and without regret.

Cathy Campbell
Hospice Bereavement Coordinator
Director of Camp Jamie

TWO SIDES OF A COIN

As infants, we learn to walk by taking baby steps. As we progress, our steps become bigger, more assured, until we are soon walking upright. Later, as children, we play a game in which we take baby steps or giant steps, forward or backward. You've probably heard the familiar phrase, "May I take two giant steps?"

The journey of grief is like that game because it is made up of a series of steps — some large, some small, some forward, and some backward from time to time. Like all journeys, there are alternate paths to take. Some are more direct than others, some more scenic, and some convoluted. But in the end, they all lead to the same destination.

When caught up in the complexities of grief, I encourage you to listen to the wise words of children. Every time I am perplexed by life's unanswered prayers, unsolved mysteries and confusion, the wisdom of children never ceases to amaze me.

One day, I was sitting with a small group of children from our bereavement camp for children. We were sitting in a circle remembering our loved ones who died. When the talking ceased and the silence filled the room, I asked, "What are you feeling?"

"Frightened," answered Jessica, whose mother had died.

"Of what?"

"That my father will die and leave me all alone."

"That could happen," I replied. "In fact, some day, he will die just like all of us will. But probably not for a long time from now. Let's think only about tomorrow, Jessica. Let's think about how wonderful tomorrow will be with your dad. Can you do that?"

"I'll try, but it won't be easy because . . . because I'm still afraid he'll die and leave me, then I'll be all alone."

"That's how I felt when my sister died," said Brittany. "We were identical twins, and I always felt as though we were two sides of the same coin. I mean, we were so much a part of each other, and now I feel that half of me is gone. That I'm only half."

We sat for a few moments watching Jessica and Brittany as they considered their fear, sadness, and emptiness. I asked if anyone had any ideas to add related to these thoughts. Derek had an idea. He had the answer.

"Brittany, you said you felt like you and your sister were two sides of the same coin and now that she's gone, you feel as if half of you is gone. But that means that half of your sister is still here."

"What?" responded Brittany, a bit bewildered.

"If part of you is gone with her, then part of her stayed behind with you. Don't you get it? It works both ways."

We may feel that half of us is gone, but we are comforted by the thought that half remained behind in our hearts and in our memories. Once we say good-bye, we are able to journey back into life, fortified with these special memories. And that is one giant step forward.

If you share your tears, and if you take that first step toward another, even if it's a small step, or if you allow that step to be the beginning of your brave walk into what you are feeling, then you can begin to defeat the power of despair. The temptation is to allow the death of your loved one to claim more than its share and leave you with anger and powerlessness. The challenge is to engage in life again with a renewed energy and embrace the new days with a gentle, welcoming spirit filled with memories.

The memories that we are left with, however, can be rainbows one day and stalking nightmares the next. When we are in a loving relationship, we make memories by just being alive together. Minute by minute, our lives create millions of impressions that are stored in our memory. It may hurt to remember. It may heal to remember. It's hard to know what the effect will be — the nature of healing is as elusive as the nature of pain. Sometimes, pain is healing. Sometimes, healing is painful.

I encourage the creation and recollection of memories because I believe in the human heart and the human spirit. I believe that we have the innate ability to change shadows into rainbows. By bringing our grief into the illuminating light of God's spirit, we are able to manage it much better and piece together all the broken pieces of our lives. Throughout all of this, your memories will sustain you — they are the reality of your love. They are the guide that will lead you home through the blackness of night and through the swirling fog of obscurity. In time, your memories will surround and comfort you. Do we ever stop grieving? No, we just call it something else — honoring and remembering.

On life's journey,
faith is nourishment,
virtuous deeds are shelter,
wisdom is the light by day
and right mindfulness
is the protection by night.

BUDDHA

Kei Gilbert
In memory of my mother's death

TOGETHER AT FIRST, SEPARATELY IN THE END

Although my mother's death was not my first experience with death, it had a profound effect on my life. My mother, Katsuko Hayashi, died at age 83 on February 15, 1999. For 50 years, she was cortisone-dependent and battled multiple illnesses, including asthma, rheumatoid arthritis, glaucoma, cataract, gout and furthermore an unknown illness which indirectly ended her life.

I had prepared myself for the inevitable, but the anticipated end came rather suddenly and unexpectedly. In 1997, when the academic program I was administering ended, I decided to work out of my home, which freed me to support my mother who lived far away. By then, she was taking more than 20 medications and had difficulty walking. My husband and I bought a house with a first-floor bedroom that would allow her to stay with us in the event my father died first. It was always her belief that she would outlive him. Those unrealized plans are now only the memory of my effort to prepare my mother toward her inevitable end.

On January 11, I made my routine transcontinental trip to help her sort through piles of "junk mail" that she never had the heart to throw away. My visits to Seattle earned me the title of being a highly-paid domestic engineer as I flew coast-to-coast to review her junk mail. She allowed only me to do this, and I had accepted that role with grace. This trip, however, had a surprise ending. On the morning I was returning to Maryland, my mother had her first incident with intestinal hemorrhaging. I found her looking frightened in the massively-soiled bathroom. My father suggested that I call the airport taxi service and go to the airport alone. My hand paged through my mother's address book for the number but instead dialed Secure Horizon, a Medicare supplemental insurance company, to see which hospital we should use. I then dialed 911. From the front of the ambulance, I assured Mom that I was with her all the way. That began our intensive journey to death, together at first, and separately in the end.

As I write now, I see that my daily calendar stops on January 11. That is the day I left Maryland for Seattle the first time that year, and the page indicates to me the beginning of the end, the end that also brought a new beginning to my life. During the first hospital stay, I rented a cot, which the hospital must have bought during World War II. It sagged so low that I could almost feel the floor. There, together in a small hospital room, I saw the pain and humiliation of being hospitalized with an illness that stripped her of privacy. Intestinal hemorrhaging meant many diagnostic tests requiring laxatives, which caused more bleeding. It was a "Catch 22" situation. My role, thus, became that of a caretaker who worked to minimize the level of humiliation. I washed her body, removed soiled towels, and sanitized the floor in an inconspicuous way that only my mother and I knew. Soon, I became aware that her body became mine, and my voice became hers. We were one body and one soul.

Mentally, Mom depended on my strength and my role as her closest "doctor" and her advocate. Over the years, I had shared with her my experiences as an educator and later as an advocate for young athletes. She somehow knew and trusted that I would protect her at this vulnerable time. One week after coming home, I flew back to Seattle to be by her side at the hospital again. I felt as if

I were a trained soldier returning for real war this time. Realizing my own physical limits, I got a room on the hospital floor that was converted into a hotel for families of hospitalized patients. The hotel bed was there for me to lie on, if not to sleep on, where I could collect my thoughts when needed. This is where I also shed tears that my mother never saw. As gentle and sensitive as Mom was, I knew I had to show strength and to monitor the care she was receiving. I could not let her see my tears, I thought.

No one had anticipated that she would not see her home again. Yet I instinctively knew. Before I left Maryland this time, I had put a set of clothes on a hanger and placed them in the closet. They were my funeral clothes that my husband later brought to Seattle. I had also bought Valentine's Day gifts for her, a heart locket and a heart bracelet, but when I was buying them, I selected a young design that my daughter, Jennifer, would also like. I somehow knew that Mom would not ever have a chance to wear them. I had a red cap embroidered with *"The Winning Child,"* which her name "Katsuko" means in Japanese. In life and in death, I wanted her to go as a winning child. The red cap traveled to Seattle and stayed above her head in the ICU. In her dying moments, I said, "Mom, remember that you are a winning child." I kept my premonition of her death to myself as a secret that was too heavy for anyone else to bear.

Back in the hospital, I did all the planning and worrying for Mom. At one point, as she was getting an angiogram of her colon, my mother yelled across the room to the doctor, "I hope my daughter isn't bothering you with too many questions." The doctor explained that if Mom hemorrhaged again, they would operate. On February 12, the same doctor removed two thirds of her colon, telling her that he was going to save her life. Before and after the surgery, I had one goal, which was to do all the monitoring for her, leaving her only with positive thoughts that would lead her body to heal. Everything seemed to go so well, or at least in our minds.

On February 14th, two days after the surgery, Mom had progressed so well that they began removing IV tubes from her. She was to be discharged the next day, and she began calling friends, telling them not to come since she would be home the next day. She was jubilant with the thought of going home, and I became lax with my job of monitoring her hospital care. I felt relaxed for the first time. Yet, Mom died the next day of massive bleeding and infection.

Between February 15th and now, I feel that I have gone through an intensive self-study course on thanatology. I learned that two people, my father and I, could have two totally different ways of handling grief over someone we loved. My father came to the ICU in a suit. When asked why he was dressed up, he said that Mom always liked to see him looking nice, and that he wanted her to remember him the way she liked. He was very much a gentleman while I was wearing the same outfit I had worn for several days. I sheltered my father from the reality of my mother's last day spent in pain and agony that resulted from medical negligence until he was ready to face them. My father allowed me to handle all the post-mortem tasks, and he devoted a week to be with a business guest from Japan. Two days before her death, unaware of her approaching death, he had promised my mother that he would take good care of his guest. My father was fulfilling the promise as if she were still alive. Perhaps, this was the last project they shared together.

I devoted my time to creating and organizing a memorial service that exemplified my mother's love for life and people. The memorial service was simple and beautiful, complete with violin, piano and voice music. It was a concert in her honor. I also answered telephone calls and cried as my mother's friends broke down, realizing that they missed their chance to bid her good-bye. My father, on the other hand, handled his grief in privacy. He and I dealt with her death in two totally different ways, each completing unfinished dreams left by my mother at the time of her death.

I learned that mourning is also a time when creative juices flow. While my father found solace through organizing his house and financial matters, I found solace through music and writing. I played the piano and sang every day. I began her biographical sketch and gardened. My father and I both found joy in watching the flowers she loved so much, and our daily phone calls were about the new life shown by the flowers and trees around us. Both separately and together, my father and I have found our ways of coming to terms with the ending of her life and the beginning of a new life without her.

Beyond all experiences, what I treasure most are the few hours I had with her before she passed away. Since the Living Will had not been filed correctly in her medical file, my mother was revived several times in the hospital room and was taken to the ICU. When the Living Will was faxed, the responsibility on her life then became my father's and mine. The surgeon asked to receive six hours to prepare her body for surgery. We agreed, not because we believed the six hours would save her life, but because my father wanted to honor the efforts of a physician that my mother trusted so much. Six hours later, the surgeon informed us that she was inoperable, and that she would die on the operating table. That, I knew from the start. I had already begun the process of preparing my mother toward the inevitable.

I firmly believe that patients who are critically ill can hear and sense their surroundings. With that belief, I began early on in the ICU to surround her thoughts with my love and the love of her family. I would say, "I love you, Mom," or "I will always stay with you here," "You can depend on me, Mom," and other similar thoughts. I learned that my son on the East Coast was upset for not visiting his grandmother in Seattle while she was alive. He was wrestling with his missed opportunity. I decided then to tell my mother in the ICU, "Brian loves you." I added, "Be Brian's guardian angel, OK?" I then began identifying all those who loved her, beginning with my daughter and her siblings, especially those who were unable to be there at the ICU. I can only assume that she heard me, and that those expressions of love supported her. Later, after her death, it became a source of comfort to my family and friends that I had relayed their love to her while she was alive.

When the decision was made to remove the hot air inside her "warming blanket," her temperature lowered drastically. I then began coaching Mom to feel comfortable about the limbo she was in. I never mentioned the word "death," since I had always sensed that she would not accept her own death. She was a fighter. I encouraged her to be strong and to depend on me since I would stay with her till the end. Her hands were so cold and discolored from bleeding that she could no longer squeeze my hand. Nevertheless, my father and I held her hands. It was probably more for our sake. She was being sent off to the new world supported by two people she loved with all her heart.

With the artificial devices removed, her respiration rate dropped further. It was during this period of time that I saw her soul fight for life, still wanting to be part of our life, near her husband, near her only child. Whenever she heard my voice or felt my hand on her forehead, her respiration rate went up. I worked to continue showing her my strength and courage. We were still a team— still one soul and one body as we had been for six days. Yet somehow, our challenge had changed before our eyes. It was no longer the courage to fight to live, but the courage to let go. We had entered a new stage, I knew. I began encouraging her to let go. I told her that her friends and family were waiting for her on the other side. It was time to move on. "We love you, but we'll be fine . . . It's OK . . . Move on," I said. She passed on very quietly and with a serene expression on her face.

My mother's death has had a tremendous impact on me. It taught me that one is never ready for the death of a loved one no matter how prepared one tries to be. It also taught me that we go through mourning in different ways, and yet we can emerge holding a legacy of the loved one close to our heart. It showed me that it is possible to offer peace to those who are dying, to those who may not be ready to die. Dying is a challenge we all face alone, but in that aloneness, it's a blessing to have a team cheering from the bench.

*We are each of us angels
with one wing.
To fly, we only need
to embrace each other.*

UNKNOWN

Ray Scheck
Pastor, Redeemer Lutheran Church

DOES GOD UNDERSTAND?
YES, AND HE CRIES.

This is a story from many years ago when I was brand new in the work and ministry of being a Roman Catholic priest. It was a mild afternoon, and the secretary handed me the phone with a look of fright on her face. On the other end of the line, I kept hearing these words . . . *Tommy is dead, Tommy is dead, Tommy is dead.* Finally, I was able to break through, and I asked the man who he was and who had died. The man's name was Tom, and his little son had just died at the hospital in Baltimore. What had happened is Tommy's mother had left her two young sons in the car while she ran up to the door to check whether it was locked. Tommy must have climbed out of his seat and somehow released the brake on the car. In only a minute, the little boy's body was under the wheel of the car rolling down the hill. His mother called 911, and the ambulance was there in no time. But Tommy's body was mortally wounded, and he died in his mom's arms on the way to the hospital.

Now the family was heading home, and the dad asked me, a priest for only a few weeks, to meet them at their home. The dad was a very intelligent administrator in the school system with a Ph.D., and when I arrived at their home, the house was already filled with many neighbors and friends. As you might imagine, I was wondering and praying over what I should say or do.

Well, the long-awaited car finally pulled up before the house, and the couple made their way into their home. I stood and watched and then I made my way to the couple. I said nothing as no words came out of my mouth. I began to cry as I held the mother. And then I made my way to the couch and sat next to the dad. He began to talk to tell me what had happened. At the hospital, another priest had been called. Perhaps out of nervousness, he told the couple that it was God's will that their son had died. Oh, all of us have said things out of being nervous. The dad looked at me as he repeated the priest's words. I said nothing. I just sat next to Tom, the dad, and held him and cried with him. I never had cried so much before as I stayed for several hours and cried and held the dad. I am sure that I said a prayer or I asked the couple and people in the room to pray with me. But that afternoon, I just listened, cried and hugged.

Now the next few days passed by as hundreds, maybe a thousand or more, came to the church where little Tommy's body lay in the sanctuary. The funeral mass and the burial in the cemetery were "well done" and there was a deep sense of God's presence with me. But Tom, Tommy's dad, was withdrawing within himself right before our eyes.

Remember I was a "rookie" as a priest. But the Lord told me to reach out to Tom and go and visit and eat with him and his family. In a mysterious way, I became so close to this dear couple and their younger son. But Tom was like a man dying within his soul. Finally, one evening, I sat next to Tom and I asked my friend if I could talk to him about Tommy. I then asked my brother whether he believed that his son was in heaven with Jesus. He nodded yes. Then I asked my brother a question that only God could have led me to ask. I asked my brother if he had died and he was in heaven, would he want his son to stop living. Tom looked at me with tears in his eyes and asked me to repeat my question. And so I repeated my question of whether he would want his son to stop living if he had died and he were the one in heaven. He said no. I then asked Tom what he thought his namesake son, Tommy, wanted to say to him from his place in heaven. Gently, I pointed out that he was breaking his son's heart in heaven because his son could see that his dad was dying within himself. I gently pointed out that his son was crying because he so wanted his dad to live his life and raise his other son and love his wife. Tom looked at me and he hugged me and he cried and cried. And I said no more.

It is over 30 years ago that this story took place, and I am no longer a Catholic priest, but now a Lutheran pastor and the father of four grown children. But what I learned 30 years ago, I have never forgotten. Sometimes, there are no words appropriate to say, and what we are called to do is to sit and hug and cry when death comes into our midst. I have cried and hugged many a man, a woman, a teen, and a child over these past years when death, like a thief, appears. What has become so clear to me is that God has taught me how to be His instrument of peace and comfort. How do we know that God understands the pain in our heart when a loved one dies? That question is answered for me in the simple words found in the Gospel of John, chapter 11, verse 35, where we read that Jesus cried when He heard that Lazarus, his friend, had died. *Jesus cried . . .* And that is how I have come to understand that God understands and cares when death appears and a loved one dies.

For me, when I prepare to reach out to someone who has lost an important relationship, I try to remember that before Jesus said any words, he cried. Before I speak to or pray for someone facing grief, I first pray so that I can be free to feel the pain of another in grief and to cry with them. And then I pray that the Holy Spirit guide my mouth when to speak and what to say.

As a pastor and a friend, I try to remember these two important words: *Jesus cried.*

Kindness is the language
which the deaf can hear
and the blind can see.

MARK TWAIN

Trisha Kiyohara
Educator

FROM GRIEF TO GRATITUDE

To grieve is a heart broken. And when grief is due to the death of a loved one, the heart is broken wide open. Emotions consume the body to the point of vacillating between intense pain to unbelievable numbness. Each grief experience is different. Everyone's healing process is unique.

The healing process can take a lifetime. I am still healing from the deaths of three significant people in my life and I expect it to take my lifetime. These three people died much too young: my beloved father at age 52, my best friend at 47 and my dear nephew at 27. Each was a victim of cancer or cancer related deterioration.

At 52 years old, my father died much too young, and at 18, I was much too young to understand mortality. We had a very close relationship, and when he died, I remained in denial and disbelief for the next two years. By the third year, my grief was finally allowed expression and manifested itself in depression, anger turned inwards. Suddenly my life had no purpose. Even if life had meaning it was surely too uncertain and too short to spend in college. I dropped out of the university in the beginning of my senior year and immersed myself into partying and discos. I drowned myself in loud music and nightlife so I wouldn't be able to hear myself question if life was worth continuing, so I wouldn't sleep and dream of my father's reappearance on my doorstep as if he had simply been vacationing in Hawaii for a few months and I could welcome him home.

At 47 years old, Vicki died much too young and I was much too young to understand that I may not grow old with my peers, with my best friend. Even in my mid-forties, I felt somewhat immune from death as if only people in their 80s and 90s need bother to think about the end of life. That someone I worked and played along side with for over 25 years could die was simply not a reality for me. Especially not someone brimming over with health, beauty and vitality as Vicki did. Not someone who loved life so profoundly. Everyone and everything Vicki encountered was cause for celebration. She had a lot to live for and never once questioned life's worth. When I heard of her cancer, there was no doubt she would beat it. And for four years she did. In the 5th year, the cancer reappeared with a vengeance. Within months the once vibrant and beautiful woman was reduced to a tiny wisp of skin, bones and morphine patches. The cancer spread into her brain and made her delusional and anxious; the morphine made her almost comatose at times. Her hospice nurse kept reassuring her family and friends that someday we would have our former Vicki "back," meaning that our memories of her former strength and vitality would eventually overpower the images left by her terrible illness. Mercifully and peacefully, she passed away in her husband's arms on a Christmas morning. I can still erupt into tears when I find a note or recipe card in her handwriting or receive a compliment on the stylish accessories and clothing she had given me over the years. Three years later, I am relieved to realize that the nurse was right. I am finally able to see our "old Vicki" smiling and laughing and smacking her lips gleefully, whether over her favorite pasta with prawns and spinach, a pair of designer shoes, or the birth of a friend's baby. The woman who loved life is still teaching me how to celebrate it even beyond her death, and even when it is hard to celebrate it without her here.

At 27 years old, my nephew Brent was much too young to die and I was much too naïve to think death would dare not prey on someone so buff and handsome, so full of noble character and so full of promise. A perfect son to my sister and brother-in-law, my sweet and softhearted nephew, my mother's beloved grandson who was the spitting image of her first love, my father, slipped into a coma after having a bone marrow transplant to cure leukemia. When Brent went in for his transplant, he, and we, expected full recovery. Up until recently he had responded to treatment with textbook perfect results until the leukemia returned and a marrow transplant was the only hope for a permanent cure. Everyone, including the doctors, had tremendous hope and a positive prognosis for him. What eventually happened is a mystery still, and a shock because Brent was supposed to live. Recently, my sister, Brent's mother, speaks of "still living daily with almost unbearable pain" when she describes the grief experience of losing her child, of losing her hopes and dreams for her oldest son. The baby I eagerly helped care for after school as a teenage aunty, the temperamental little boy I watched grow into a calm, polite and soft-hearted teenager, and the generous loving adult I was so proud to call my nephew was gone from our family gatherings. The extraordinarily responsible and mature young man who always shunned smoking, alcohol, drugs, and even reckless spending and driving, was stopped short in his tracks, regardless. Evidently death doesn't discriminate against the young, the healthy or the good.

Two months ago our family discovered just how generous, kind and noble Brent's character had been when a former co-worker of Brent's, and stranger to our family, told my mother about an incident that happened several Christmases before Brent's death, several years before his leukemia struck. Another employee, a single mother with several young children, was to receive a lay-off notice just weeks before Christmas. When Brent heard this was about to happen, his heart ached and he asked his employer to consider some mercy, being that it was Christmas and there would be children affected. The employer wasn't sympathetic so Brent took several thousand dollars from his own paycheck and savings and gave it as a Christmas gift to this fellow soon-to-be unemployed coworker so her family could still enjoy Christmas. Brent never told anyone in the family what he had done; only recently were we made aware of this act of amazing sensitivity and kindness.

When I heard this story of Brent, my understanding of a potential aspect of the grieving process became clear: grief could be balanced with, and in time perhaps even replaced by, gratitude. Gratitude that someone as noble and kind as Brent had been given to our family for as long as he had been, if only for 27 years. Gratitude that Brent had not died from the emergency cesarean delivery or the severe asthma attacks he had as a baby but was allowed to grow into young adulthood. Gratitude that there was nothing but love and affection between him and every family member and friends he possessed. It was standing room only at his memorial service and until then, even his parents hadn't been aware of how many lives he had touched. The emotional impact of the numbers who came to pay their respects to such a young person just beginning life on his own was absolutely overwhelming. One by one, a number of people stood up to share their stories of Brent's kindness to them and the impact he made on their lives. How can I not be utterly grateful for not only having known such an individual but also to be able to call him family?

When I contemplate how the perspective of gratitude helps me in my grief, I am reminded of a Bible verse to "be thankful in everything." Many years ago while still struggling to understand my father's early death, this verse was pretty hard to swallow. Be thankful for everything? How could I be thankful for losing my father when he was much too young to die and I was much too young to lose a dad? But in reading the verse again and again, I realized that the pivotal word was not "for" but rather "in": be thankful IN everything. Even when we can't be thankful for the circumstance. Even when we are hurting. As difficult as this exercise of thankfulness is, with practice and maturity, it has become a little less foreign to me with every trial and loss in this journey of life. Practicing gratitude, whether consciously or unconsciously, I realize now how I eventually came to terms with my father's untimely death. When I hear of others speak of difficult, even estranged relationships with their fathers, I am so grateful that the relationship between Dad and me was close and loving. When I hear of others struggling to believe in the unconditional and steadfast love of a Heavenly Father because of how their own earthly fathers failed to show such love to them as children, I am grateful that my dad gave me such a positive image of a father's love, mercy and help so I could have a positive relationship with God. When I think of my childhood, I am grateful that I had a humorous and sometimes goofy dad who made everyday events fun and happy. My memory book of our relationship may have only spanned 18 years, but it is packed to overflowing with good times and loving feelings. I realize this is something to truly appreciate when so many adults my age seem to still be trying to gather but just one page of good memories even as their difficult and distant fathers grow into old age.

As for my grief over losing Vicki, my dear friend, there's not a single day when I don't think of her in some way. I am surrounded by the many gifts from her and am grateful not just for her material gifts of which she was generous to a fault, but even more so, for the gifts of her personality, style and spirit. For a while I would be burdened with the thought that I would likely never again have such a close friend. Our friendship was honed and smoothed by almost three decades. We had seen each other through many rites of passage. I felt great sorrow that I lost the only long and close friendship I would probably ever have, apart from my marriage to my husband. At some point however, my sorrow was replaced with the realization that our long and wonderful friendship was not a right to demand of life, but a gift and a privilege that not many people, especially I, could expect to receive. I say, "especially I," because although my friends and acquaintances are many, it is not my nature to cultivate genuinely deep and longtime friendships. I realized that our extraordinary friendship was not because of anything I had done, but truly because of Vicki's faithful nurturing of our relationship and the sheer unconditional generosity of her spirit. It was Vicki who always remembered my birthday, even when I was always late for hers, and it was she who called to remind me we should get together for dinner when the demands of my career and disorganized personal life often made a blur of time and space. She didn't forget me, even as I neglected her. Now that she is gone, I remember her every day, and always with gratitude for the gift of such a friendship that comes to but a few. How can I not feel grateful for a commodity so precious, yet so undeserved?

I don't think it's possible to come to this point of gratitude immediately after the loss of a loved one. I suppose this comes only at the stage when one comes face to face with a choice: either to continue in the pain of grief or move towards healing. At some point in each of my grief experiences, I no longer wanted to feel loss and shed tears at every memory of my beloved deceased. My broken heart was ready to begin the healing process. Whether consciously or subconsciously during each grief experience, I felt that my father, Vicki and Brent all deserved better. They deserved to be remembered in joy and gratefulness for their lives. There is no better way to honor the worth of someone's life than to express sincere and deep gratitude for it. Since grieving my father's death and coming to a place of constant gratitude for his life, I no longer ask the purpose of my existence. Death gives purpose to life and the purpose is clear: to live in such a way that others, too, might be grateful that I lived.

The gratitude is
the heart's memory.

FRENCH PROVERB

$\mathcal{B}$OOKS, MUSIC, AND FILMS
$\mathcal{S}$UPPORT GROUPS

This section lists some interesting and
useful resources. I hope the list will
give you a head start in your search
for the tools that give you comfort
and understanding. The Internet has
wonderful listings of books, music
and support groups.

*The greatest discovery
of my generation is
that a human being
can alter his life
by altering his
attitudes of mind.*

WILLIAM JAMES

Books

GENERAL READING:

Albom, Mitch. (1997). *Tuesdays with Morrie.* Doubleday.

Callanan, Maggie and Kelley, Patricia. (1992). *Final Gifts.* New York: Bantam Books.

Doka, Kenneth - Editor. (2000). *Living with Grief, Children, Adolescents, and Loss.* Washington, D.C: Hospice Foundation of America.

Gibran, Kahlil. *The Prophet.* New York: Random House

Kastenbaum, Robert. (2000). *The Psychology of Death.* New York, NY: Springer Publishing.

Kübler-Ross, Elisabeth. (1969). *On Death and Dying.* New York, NY: MacMillan.

Kübler-Ross, Elisabeth. (1981). *Living with Death and Dying.* New York, NY: MacMillan.

Kushner, Harold S. (1981). *When Bad Things Happen to Good People.* New York: Avon Books.

Prend, Ashley Davis. (1997). *Transcending Loss, Understanding the Life Long Impact on Grief and How to Make it Meaningful.* Berkley Pub Group

Welshons, John E. (1999). *Awakening from Grief: Finding the Road Back to Joy.* New Jersey: Open Heart Communications.

EASY READING:

Bell Mathis, Sharon. (1986). *The Hundred Penny Box.* New York: Penguin Group

Bird Baylor. (1987). *When Clay Sings.* New York: Aladdin Paperbacks

Bird Baylor. (1995). *I'm in Charge of Celebrations.* New York: Aladdin Paperbacks

Buscaglia, Leo. (1982). *The Fall of Freddie the Leaf.* New Jersey: Slack, Inc.

De Saint-Exupery, Antoine. (2000). *The Little Prince*. New York: Hardcourt Brace Trade.

Le Shan, Eda. (1976). *Learning to Say Good-bye*. New York: MacMillan: New York

Silverstein, Shel. (1986). *The Giving Tree*. New York: Harpercollins Juvenile Books.

White, E. B. (1999). *Charlotte's Web*. New York: Harpercollins Juvenile Books.

Soothing Music

The Enchanted Forest	Melodies of Japan: lyrical flute music (James Galway)
The Wind Beneath My Wings	Soothing flute music (James Galway)
Winter's Crossing	A story, told through music, of the Irish immigrating to the United States in the 1800s (James Galway)
Music of Hikari Oe, (1 and 2)	Piano, flute and violin. Hikari Oe, the son of a Nobel Prize winner, is autistic. He communicates with the outside world through his music. His composition is very peaceful.
Romanza	Voice music by Andrea Bocelli, who is gifted, inspirational, and blind
Sacred Songs	Andrea Bocelli
Sogno	Andrea Bocelli

Cousteau's Dream	A benefit album for Cousteau's Society; music donated by various composers
If I Could Tell You	Music composed by Yanni
Lift up Your Hearts	Religious voice music (Christian hymns) sung by Denise Morency Gannon.
Saving Trees	Dulcimer music by Sam Rizzetta. Track 9 is dedicated to his deceased mother. (rizzetta@aol.com)
Shepherd Moons	Voice music by Enya
Whisper From the Mirror	Piano music by Keiko Matsui

Films of Interest

ON DEATH, AGING AND RELIGIONS:

Let Sorrow Find Words. Produced by Soras Corporation. (www.soras.com). A 90-minute informative and heart-felt film on grief.

On Our Own Terms, Moyers on Dying. Public Affairs Television, Inc. Four programs on the stories of dying individuals.

Ponette. Fox Lorber. ISBN: 1-57252-258-5. A French movie about a little girl whose mother dies. Touching. Delightful

Religions of the World. Schlessinger Media. ISBN: 1-57225-246-4. Includes Buddhism, Catholicism, Hinduism, Islam, Judaism, and Protestantism.

Stealing Time, the New Science of Aging. PBS Home Video. ISBN: 0-7806-2455-6. A set of three tapes on man's quest for immortality and the science of aging.

INSPIRATIONAL:

Finding Forrester, co-directed by Sean Connery, Laurence Mark, and Rhonda Tollefson. A film involving an unlikely friendship that develops between a recluse novelist and an inner-city high school athlete with the gift for writing.

Mr. Holland's Opus, directed by Stephen Herek. (Hollywood Pictures. ISBN: 0-7888-0556-8) A film on a high school music teacher who battles and wins against all odds.

Remember the Titans, directed by Boaz Yakin. A true story of a high school coach who coaches the Titans' first integrated football team in the 1960s, where the winning is not only on the field but in their hearts.

Rudy, directed by David Anspaugh. A story based on the life of a working-class boy whose goal is to play football at University of Notre Dame. Despite all obstacles, he achieves his goal through sheer desire, work and commitment.

Stand and Deliver, directed by Ramón Menéndez. A true story about an inspiring Los Angeles math teacher who takes a group of high school students well beyond expectations.

Support Groups

The following list of Internet sites will give you a head start in finding a support group or other sources for further learning.

ADEC (Association for death education and counseling): http://www.adec.org

Ashley Foundation (a foundation devoted to teenagers facing death) http://www.theashleyfoundation.org